Mergers & Acquisitions

Will You Overpay?

Mergers & Acquisitions

Will You Overpay?

Joseph H. Marren

DOW JONES-IRWIN   Homewood, Illinois   60430

ISBN 0-87094-581-5

Library of Congress Catalog Card No. 84–72811

Printed in the United States of America

1 2 3 4 5 6 7 8 9 0 **K** 2 1 0 9 8 7 6 5

To my wife, Joan

Preface

Unquestionably the most difficult decision that an executive faces in negotiating an acquisition involves the pricing issue. The decision is difficult because there are so many factors to consider—the future profitability of the target, expected synergies if any, complex tax rules, alternative legal forms of effecting the transaction, accounting considerations, etc. To date there have been numerous articles and texts written which have been targeted at certain of these factors. However, the author believes this book is the first attempt to integrate the key legal, tax, accounting, and financial concepts into a unified approach for analyzing a target company.

The book began as my thesis at New York University's Graduate School of Business. However, the approach detailed in the book is based on five years of practical experience analyzing acquisitions and divestitures for American Maize-Products Company. American Maize is a diversified conglomerate which has interests in corn wet milling, cigars, and the retailing of building materials. During the 1979–84 period American Maize was directed by a president and a chairman whose backgrounds were not financial in nature. Thus the approach advocated in the book distills complex concepts down to relevant information that a non-financially oriented decision maker can use in making the pricing decision.

The book is written principally for top management and professionals involved in the acquisition process including lawyers, accountants, bankers, consultants, and intermediaries. However, it should also prove worthwhile reading for individuals concerned with valuing companies including investors, security analysts, and arbitrageurs.

Acknowledgments

I have received a great deal of assistance in preparing this book. Top management and the corporate staff at American Maize-Products Company including Bill Ziegler, Chairman of the Board and Chief Executive Officer; Les Liabo, President and Chief Operating Officer; Al Edly, Vice President-Finance; Don McNicol, Secretary and General Counsel; Bob Britton, Treasurer; Ed Norris, Controller; and Tom Fisher, Tax Manager have made innumerable intellectual and practical contributions to my thinking. However, I am especially indebted to Bill Rawlings, former President of American Maize-Products, and Kip Koons, Vice President-Corporate Planning & Development, for their rigorous review of my ideas.

Outside of American-Maize, Charlie Phillipin, a partner in Coopers & Lybrand's, Stamford, Connecticut, office offered a number of useful thoughts on an early draft of the manuscript and, George E. Pinches, Professor of Finance at Kansas University, provided a comprehensive critique of a late draft. Bob Howell, Clinical Professor of Management and Accounting at New York University and President of Howell Management Corporation, provided some perceptive insights on the format of the book. My brother, Bernie Marren, Jr., Tax Attorney—Clabir Corporation, has helped refine my thinking, particularly in the tax area, and has been a continuing source of new ideas. Moreover, his review of the manuscript yielded numerous productive comments.

The book would never have seen the light of day without the diligent efforts of my "superstar" secretary, Rose Picarazzi. Preliminary design work for the jacket was done by the advertising department at Lloyd Home & Building Center for which I am grateful.

In large measure this book is the product of my parents' efforts. Everything that I have achieved is directly related to the values they instilled and the example they set. My dad was the finest businessman I have ever known. The real world education he gave me was a necessary prerequisite for writing this book.

Finally, I would like to thank my wife Joan for her patience with what seemed like a never ending project, constant encouragement, useful comments, and loving support.

Contents

SECTION THREE

SECTION FOUR

SECTION FIVE

APPENDIXES

Section One

Introduction

Chapter 1

Three Basic Questions

1.1 THE PURCHASING DECISION— CONDITIONED EXPECTATIONS

How many times has the key decision maker in a corporation made purchases of products for personal use? The answer is thousands. In most of those purchases the executive physically examined the merchandise to be purchased and formed an opinion as to its value. Similarly, the key decision maker has made numerous major purchase decisions in his executive capacity regarding equipment, supplies, services, and so forth, that were normally made based on an informed judgment about their value.

Achieving an informed judgment from a financial standpoint means an executive must answer three basic questions:

1. **Cost.** What will the asset cost?
2. **Return.** What return can we expect if we make the purchase? (This question is often phrased in terms of cash flow, payback period, net present value, or return on investment.)
3. **Risk.** What is the probability of achieving the expected return?

Generally, an executive answers these questions by requesting comparative bids, internal studies, research reports, industry information, consultant's opinions, or capital budgeting analyses. The last type of analysis is standard procedure at most large concerns for purchases over a certain dollar limit. It involves analyzing in detail the factors that influence the financial consequences of an investment decision.

However, when the executive must evaluate the price to be paid for a particular business, the process changes. Typically, the executive initially reviews the strategic aspects of making the acquisition. Assuming the executive decides that the acquisition fits into the company's strategy, how does the executive come to an informed judgment about the target company's value? If the executive is associated with an unsophisticated company, the historical financial results of the target are reviewed and an offer is made based on (1) some multiple of historical earnings or (2) the book value of the company. If the executive is from a more sophisticated organization, its financial department and/or investment banker puts together financial forecasts that influence the executive in negotiating an agreement on price.

In either of the acquisition settings described, the decision maker does not achieve the same level of comfort in estimating the value of the goods to be received (the target business) that can be achieved in other purchase situations. The trouble lies with the fact that the executive does not receive satisfactory answers to the cost, return, and risk questions. This is in large measure due to the complexity of the alternative forms of business acquisitions. In other purchase situations the buyer is faced with the following: Do we want to pay $X for a specified good or service? If the good is a tangible asset, the buyer normally understands that the acquiring company can take full tax depreciation deductions on that asset over some time period. In evaluating a business acquisition the decision maker has numerous alternative ways to effect the transaction that are only vaguely understood. Furthermore, each alternative method of effecting the transaction has tax ramifications that are beyond comprehension for most executives in any reasonable time frame. Since the decision maker is faced with this situation a few times, at most, in a lifetime, a normal reaction is to try to fit the acquisition into the standard purchase mold: We will pay you $X for your company! In that situation the executive believes that whatever $X is, it represents the true cost of acquiring the target company.

1.2 THE COST PROBLEM—ALTERNATE ACQUISITION METHODS

The trouble with putting an acquisition in the standard purchase mold is that it may not lead to an understanding of the cost of the transaction. The standard purchase mold only applies if the acquiring company is making one particular type of acquisition—an Asset Acquisition. If any of the five other methods of consummating a deal is utilized, in many instances the decision maker does not understand the true cost of the acquisition to the acquiring company.

The six basic alternative tax methods for consummating an acquisition are:

1. Asset Acquisition.
2. 338 Transaction.
3. Stock Acquisition.
4. Type A Reorganization.
5. Type B Reorganization.
6. Type C Reorganization.

A brief description of each of these methods follows. Chapter 3 contains a detailed discussion of each method, their various permutations, and the appropriate tax treatment for the buyer and seller under each method.

1. **Asset Acquisition.** In an Asset Acquisition the acquiring company purchases a part or all of the assets of the target company for cash, stock, securities, or other consideration. Payment is made to the target company which remains in existence subsequent to the transaction. The transaction is generally a taxable sale by the target company of its assets. However, if the target company adopts a plan of complete liquidation and distributes all of its assets (generally cash), no gain or loss will be recognized on the asset sale by the target company. Nevertheless, the shareholders of the target will recognize gain or loss upon the distribution of proceeds in complete liquidation of their interests.

2. **338 Transaction.** The acquiring company purchases the stock of the target from the target's shareholders for cash, stock, securities, or other consideration and elects pursuant to Internal Revenue Code (IRC) Section 338 by the 15th day of the ninth month after the month of acquisition to treat the transaction as if the target company sold its assets for a price equal to their fair market value. This transaction is a taxable sale by the target's shareholders of their stock.

3. **Stock Acquisition.** The acquiring company purchases the stock of the target for cash, stock, securities, or other consideration. This transaction is a taxable sale by the target's shareholders of their stock.

4. **Type A Reorganization.** In a Type A Reorganization the acquiring company purchases the target through merger or consolidation. The acquiring company pays for the acquisition by exchanging various consideration—voting or nonvoting common or preferred stock, cash, securities, or other consideration. Any combination of these kinds of consideration are acceptable as long as greater than 50 percent of the total consideration paid is some form of equity security. The transaction is nontaxable to

all parties if only equity securities are used by the acquiring company. If cash, securities, or other consideration are exchanged, the target's stockholders will be taxed to some extent. (Note: In tax lingo, this cash, securities, or other consideration received by the seller is generally called boot.)

5. **Type B Reorganization.** In a Type B Reorganization the acquiring company uses its own voting stock to purchase the stock of the target. The transaction is nontaxable to all parties involved in the transaction.

6. **Type C Reorganization.** In a Type C Reorganization the acquiring company purchases substantially all of the target company's assets with its own voting stock. In certain instances the acquiring company can give as part of the consideration a minor amount of cash, nonvoting stock, securities, or other consideration. Generally, this transaction is nontaxable to all parties involved.

Each of the various acquisition methods described above can result in significant differences in the true economic cost of the acquisition to the acquiring company. This causes problems when, as all too often happens in acquisitions, the decision maker reaches an "agreement in principal" with the seller as to the purchase price and the method of acquisition before the decision maker has the acquiring company's legal and tax experts review the proposal and comment as to its economic burden. This situation is typical because (*a*) the buyer is looking to make a deal and (*b*) the seller generally knows its tax situation extremely well and starts all discussions stating that it wants the transaction effected using a particular acquisition method, which just happens to minimize taxes for the seller.

1.3 RISK AND RETURN— THE BUSINESS FORECAST

It was mentioned earlier that in sophisticated organizations it is the norm that financial forecasts are put together to analyze the target company. The fact that forecasts are done is not important in and of itself. What is important is the discipline of having the person who will have operating responsibility for the target company get comfortable with the assumptions used to generate any earnings forecast. In order to facilitate this effort the acquiring company should draw on the necessary talent within the organization to put together a realistic model. One often cited reason for acquisitions failing to live up to expectations is management's unfamiliarity with the target's business. Therefore, if a target is in an unrelated industry, the acquiring company should enlist knowledgeable advisors to help frame the assumptions for the model.

Without such support, management will often overestimate the profitability of the target ("grass is always greener" phenomenom). Mobil's $1.86 billion acquisition in the mid-1970s of Marcor, the parent of Montgomery Ward and Container Corp. of America, has been identified by a number of commentators as an example of an acquisition where the acquiring company clearly did not understand the businesses it was acquiring.

A second significant reason for preparing a detailed business forecast is to solidify the acquiring company's thinking as to what it would do with the target company once it is acquired. Going through a detailed financial forecast forces the acquirer to think through the ramifications of the acquisition. A classic example of an acquisition that was not well thought out was Pan Am's acquisition of National Airlines for $400 million in 1980. Pan Am was attracted to National because Pan Am had few domestic routes while National had few foreign routes. A merger of the two operations would presumably enable Pan Am to use National's routes to feed Pan Am's overseas routes. However, labor strife sidetracked management's attention for almost two years before the domestic routes were rescheduled to feed the overseas flights.

In preparing the business forecast, alternative assumptions about key operating variables need to be made to give the decision maker a feeling for the risk involved in the acquisition. These assumptions should attempt to portray realistic possibilities based on a detailed review of the target company's industry trends and conditions. Two acquisitions that have been cited as instances where the acquiring company did not appreciate the downside potential in the industry were Atlantic Richfield's purchase of Anaconda for $700 million in 1977 and Sohio's purchase of Kennecott Copper for $1.77 billion in 1981. Neither acquirer saw the impending imbalance between supply and demand for copper that sent prices plummeting. The result for both companies was a financial disaster. Significant expenditures were required to lower operating costs to remain competitive at a time when the acquisitions were not producing any profits.

An important part of the financial analysis should be reviewing the impact of the acquisition on the acquiring company's liquidity and overall financial strength. Although the acquiring company may be financially able to consummate the acquisition today, what will the acquirer's balance sheet look like a year from now, or two, given the acquiring company's and target company's respective financial forecasts? Two acquisitions that had disastrous results because of management's failure to adequately analyze the impact of the acquisition on the acquiring company's liquidity and overall financial strength were Wickes Cos.'s acquisition of Gamble-Skogmo and Baldwin United Corp.'s purchase of Mortgage Guaranty Insurance Corp. (MGIC). Both companies were forced into Chapter 11 as a direct result of their acquisitions.

1.4 ORGANIZATION OF THE BOOK

The author's primary goal in writing this book is to describe an approach for analyzing a target company that will generate relevant information that an unsophisticated decision maker can use in making both the pricing decision for the target company and the decision on the manner of effecting the transaction. The approach seeks to answer the three basic financial questions: (1) What will the acquisition cost? (2) What return can the acquiring company expect if it makes the acquisition? (3) What risk is involved in achieving the expected return? The approach consists of two separate analyses: (*a*) cost analysis and (*b*) risk and return analysis. Both analyses should be completed before the decisions on the price to be paid or the method of acquisition are made.

The **cost analysis** produces summarized information on the real cost of effecting a transaction at various purchase prices using different acquisition methods. Failure to wait for completion of this analysis will result in the decision maker having to attempt to backtrack in negotiations as he learns of the economic burden of consummating the deal in a certain manner. The cost analysis starts from the point of view that the decision maker understands the simplest form of acquisition—the Asset Acquisition. All other prices and acquisition methods are then related to it.

The **risk and return analysis** is designed to produce information on the returns that the acquiring company can expect to achieve under different operating scenarios given various purchase prices. The analysis produces this data through an integrated computer model that includes income statements, balance sheets, cash flow forecasts at different levels within the target company, and numerous supporting schedules. There are a number of computer models available today that would generate these schedules. What makes this acquisition model different? Three things set this model apart from others: (1) the linkage between the business forecast and relevant tax factors, (2) the degree of integration that exists among all schedules, and (3) model results are presented in a format that is exceptionally easy to understand.

Following the description of the two analyses, a realistic example is reviewed. In this example the two analyses are examined in detail, including the formats for presenting the results.

This book is aimed at analyzing the pricing decision for the vast majority of acquisitions wherein the acquiring company purchases 100 percent of the target's business. It does not attempt to deal fully with acquisitions of less than 100 percent interest or acquisitions consummated in an unusual manner. This book is also not intended as a technical manual on taxes or finance. Discussion on either topic is limited to the extent deemed relevant to understanding the pricing decision.

An outline of the organization of this book follows:

		Chapters
Section One	**Introduction**	1
Section Two	**Cost Analysis**	2–5
Section Three	**Risk and Return Analysis**	6
Section Four	**An Example—Case of Mareight Corporation**	7
Section Five	**Conclusion**	8
Appendix A	**Discounted Cash Flow Techniques**	
Appendix B	**Basic Tax Rules**	
Appendix C	**Accounting for an Acquisition**	

1.5 THE PRICE OF VICTORY

Many managements will undoubtedly deal with the valuations resulting from the approach advocated in this book in the same manner that they have dealt with other valuation analyses. In the heat of battle they will decide to disregard the "numbers" and make a higher offer to outbid a rival and close a deal. The financial newspapers are filled daily with stories of top management making that final step necessary to close the deal.

- Standard Oil Co. of California outbid a number of rivals including Atlantic Richfield Co.; Allied Corp.; a group led by Mesa Petroleum; and a leveraged buyout group headed by Kohlberg, Kravis, Roberts & Co. for Gulf Corp. offering $80 a share early in 1984. The $13.4 billion transaction was the largest merger in corporate history at that time.
- United Technologies and J. Ray McDermott fought dramatically in an effort to gain control of Babcock & Wilcox a few years ago. They drove the price of the stock from about $35 to $65 before McDermott prevailed.
- Exxon in a preemptive $1.2 billion bid paid Reliance Electric's shareholders twice the company's market value in 1979. Exxon believed that the electric equipment maker had developed a revolutionary product that would significantly raise the efficiency of most electric motors.

Whether these and other controversial acquisition decisions were motivated by ego and made regardless of the numbers is an open question. However, no matter what the rationale, to the extent that the acquiring company's management overpaid for the target, it was at the acquiring company's shareholders' expense. The author hopes that the analytical approach in this book is persuasive enough to convince some managers to make acquisition pricing decisions with their head instead of just their emotions.

REFERENCE FOR CHAPTER 1

Fisher, Anne B. "The Decade's Worst Mergers," *Fortune,* April 30, 1984, pp. 263–70.

Section Two

Cost Analysis

Introduction

Section Two is devoted to answering the question "What will an acquisition cost?" The section consists of Chapters 2 through 5. In Chapter 2 we explore some basic concepts of acquisition cost including the importance of the tax basis of assets and the categorization of the six acquisition methods. Chapter 3 describes in detail those six acquisition methods and their tax treatment. Chapter 4 lays out a theoretical framework for calculating the real economic cost and proceeds in a transaction and contains a review of the nontax factors that influence the buyer and the seller. Chapter 5 proposes an analytical approach for comparing the costs and proceeds under different acquisition methods and purchase prices.

Chapter 2

Fundamental Concepts

2.1 INTRODUCTION

The purpose of this chapter is to highlight the economic importance of the tax basis of the assets of the target business and categorize the six acquisition methods according to how they handle this consideration. Furthermore, this chapter will explore the difference between taxable and nontaxable acquisition methods and the distinctions between stock and asset deals.

2.2 ECONOMICS OF TAX BASIS OF ASSETS

The importance of the tax basis of the assets of the target business will be highlighted by discussing some examples. However, before turning to these examples it is worthwhile to review some basic tax concepts. Generally a corporate or individual taxpayer's original **basis** in any property is equal to its cost,[1] while the **adjusted basis** of the property at any point in time is equal to its original cost adjusted for certain items.[2] Common adjustment items include depreciation, amortization, capital expenditures, earnings and profits, stock dividends, and distributions representing return of capital.

EXAMPLE 2A *ABC Corporation starts up manufacturing operations in 1976 and purchases land, buildings, and machines A and B. Over the years the business grows and prospers, although no further assets are purchased. At December 31, 1984, the company has property, land, and equipment recorded for tax purposes as follows:*

	Cost	Accumulated Depreciation	Adjusted Tax Basis	Assumed Fair Market Value	Difference
Land	$ 50	$ 0	$ 50	$110	$ 60
Buildings and improvements	150	30	120	180	60
Equipment A	100	80	20	10	(10)
Equipment B	200	150	50	300	250
	$500	$260	$240	$600	$360

XYZ Corporation is presently considering purchasing ABC. If the tax basis of the assets is unchanged in the acquisition of ABC, the acquiring company may only continue to depreciate the adjusted tax basis of the buildings and improvements and the equipment. Furthermore, these assets can only be depreciated using depreciation methods and useful lives in effect when the assets were placed in service (see paragraph B.402). However, if the tax basis of the assets is changed to reflect their fair market values, the acquiring company can take ACRS depreciation deductions based on these fair market values. (See paragraph B.401 for a description of ACRS depreciation.)

Let us see what this means in actual terms over a five-year period. We will assume that the buildings and improvements are currently being depreciated using straight-line depreciation and will be fully depreciated in 12 more years, and the machinery will be fully depreciated using the straight-line method over the next two years. We will disregard for the moment the effects of investment credit and depreciation recapture.

Depreciation Deductions Assuming No Change in Basis

	1985	1986	1987	1988	1989
Buildings and improvements	$10	$10	$10	$10	$10
Equipment A	10	10			
Equipment B	25	25			
Total Deductions	$45	$45	$10	$10	$10

ACRS Depreciation Deductions Assuming Basis Changed to Equal Fair Market Value* (All Figures Rounded)

	Fair Market Value	ACRS Class of Property	1985	1986	1987	1988	1989
Buildings and improvements	$180	18-year	$16	$16	$14	$13	$11
Equipment A	10	5-ycar	2	2	2	2	2
Equipment B	300	5-year	45	66	63	63	63
	$490		$63	$84	$79	$78	$76

*Deductions calculated using table in paragraph B.40lb.

Comparative Analysis of After-Tax Difference of Depreciation Deductions under No Change in Basis versus New Cost Basis Method

	1985	1986	1987	1988	1989
Total deductions assuming no change in basis method	$ 45	$ 45	$ 10	$ 10	$ 10
Total deductions assuming new cost basis method	63	84	79	78	76
Difference	(18)	(39)	(69)	(68)	(66)
Assumed tax rate—50%	× 50%	× 50%	× 50%	× 50%	× 50%
After-tax difference	$ (9)	$ (20)	$ (35)	$ (34)	$ (33)

If we assumed a 10 percent discount rate, the present value of the difference in after-tax cost for the two alternative categories of acquisition methods is $95. Given that the assumed total market value of the assets was $600, this figure represents 16 percent of the fair market value of the assets.

Two points need to be stressed about this hypothetical example. First, due to the significant amount of inflation in the United States during the 1970s and 1980s, a large difference between the fair market value of assets and their adjusted tax basis is the norm rather than the exception. Second, the enactment of ACRS significantly increased the difference to be expected in depreciation deduction calculations because this cost recovery system substantially reduced the period over which costs would be recovered for most assets.

The following example explores the less typical situation wherein the fair market values of a company's assets are less than their adjusted tax basis.

EXAMPLE 2B *Same facts as Example 2A except the company's assets are valued at below their adjusted tax basis:*

	Adjusted Tax Basis	Assumed Fair Market Value	Difference
Land	$ 50	$ 40	$(10)
Buildings and improvements	120	90	(30)
Equipment A	20	15	(5)
Equipment B	50	40	(10)
	$240	$185	$(55)

In this example it is fairly obvious that the acquiring company will get larger depreciation deductions if it uses an acquisition method that does not change the tax basis of the assets of the acquired business. The calculations that substantiate this notion are as follows:

ACRS Depreciation Deductions Assuming Basis Changed to Equal Fair Market Value

	Fair Market Value	ACRS Class of Property	1985	1986	1987	1988	1989
Buildings and improvements	$ 90	18-year	$ 8	$ 8	$ 7	$ 6	$ 5
Equipment A	15	5-year	2	3	3	3	3
Equipment B	40	5-year	6	9	8	8	8
	$145		$16	$20	$18	$17	$16

Comparative Analysis of After-Tax Difference of Depreciation Deductions under No Change in Basis versus New Cost Basis Method

	1985	1986	1987	1988	1989
Total deductions assuming no change in basis method	$ 45	$ 45	$ 10	$ 10	$ 10
Total deductions assuming new cost basis method	16	20	18	17	16
Difference	29	25	(8)	(7)	(6)
Assumed tax rate—50%	× 50%	× 50%	× 50%	× 50%	× 50%
After-tax difference	$ 15	$ 13	$ (4)	$ (4)	$ (3)

If we assumed a 10 percent discount rate, the present value of the difference in after-tax cost for the two alternative categories of acquisition methods is $17. Given that the total value of the assets purchased was $185, the difference in the after-tax cost of the two alternate approaches represents a significant 9 percent.

The message that the two examples are trying to convey should be clear. There is real economic significance in the choice between an acquisition method that results in a new tax basis for the assets of the target and one that does not.

2.3   TWO CATEGORIES OF ACQUISITIONS

Generally, the tax basis of the assets of the acquired business is the tax consideration with the most significant economic consequences for the acquiring corporation. For that reason the various acquisition methods are categorized as to how they handle this consideration. The six acquisition methods are divided into two categories: (1) acquisition methods that result in a new cost basis for the assets of the acquired business and (2) acquisition methods that leave the tax basis of the assets of the acquired business unchanged. The schedule below indicates how the acquisition methods are categorized. As indicated previously the various methods are discussed in detail in Chapter 3.

3.2   New Cost Basis Acquisition Methods
    3.201   Asset Acquisition
    3.202   338 Transaction
3.3   No Change in Basis Acquisition Methods
    3.301   Stock Acquisition
    3.302   Type A Reorganization
    3.303   Type B Reorganization
    3.304   Type C Reorganization

2.4   LEGAL AND TAX FRAMEWORK

Even though we have identified the tax basis of the assets of the target as the consideration that will drive our economic analysis, we must be cognizant of the legal and tax classifications of the various acquisition methods. The matrix below indicates that acquisitions (1) fall into two broad legal categories that represent alternative legal forms for effecting a transaction and (2) can be characterized as either taxable or nontaxable transactions. The characterization of a transaction as taxable or nontaxable relates solely to the taxability of the transaction to the selling corporation in the case of an asset deal or to the selling stockholders in a stock transaction (see Illustration 1).

Illustration 1

		Tax	
		Taxable Acquisition	*Nontaxable Acquisition*
Legal	Acquisition of Stock	• 338 Transaction • Stock Acquisition	• Type A Reorganization • Type B Reorganization
	Acquisition of assets	• Asset Acquisition	• Type C Reorganization

2.401   Stock versus Asset Deals

Shareholders of a company who are looking to sell their company can effect a sale in only two ways: they can (1) sell their stock (including effecting a statutory merger or consolidation), or (2) arrange for the target company to sell its assets to the acquiring company. The buyer's and seller's economic perspectives and the nontax factors that influence the structuring of a transaction are discussed in Chapter 4.

In a **Stock Acquisition** the acquiring company buys the stock of the target company from the individual shareholders of the target company. In situations where the target company is a wholly owned subsidiary of a larger corporation, the sole stockholder that the acquiring company has to deal with is the parent company. However, in cases where the target is a public company, the acquiring company must deal with a large group of shareholders. In such circumstances the acquiring company addresses these stockholders by making a tender offer. The Securities and Exchange Commission promulgates rules and regulations regarding such tender offers. Although the Stock Acquisition transaction occurs between the acquiring company and the target company's shareholders, the target company's management is generally deeply involved in negotiating the form and terms of the transaction. The only instance where this would not be the case is where an acquiring company makes an unfriendly tender offer for a public company.

A **Statutory Merger** occurs when two or more corporations combine in such a way that one of the combining corporations remains in existence while the other participating corporations disappear. Statutory mergers are effected pursuant to state merger statutes. All states have enacted such statutes into their general corporation laws.

EXAMPLE 2C *ABC Corporation is merged into XYZ Corporation. ABC Corporation disappears, and XYZ Corporation is the surviving corporation.*

A **consolidation** is effected when two or more corporations are combined into a new corporation. The new corporation sometimes comes into existence by operation of law and sometimes it must be formed. Which rule is operative depends on the applicable state law.

EXAMPLE 2D *ABC Corporation and XYZ Corporation are combined in a statutory consolidation. Both ABC and XYZ disappear, and an entirely new corporation results (assuming that it is formed by operation of law).*

In an **Asset Acquisition** the acquiring company purchases a part or all of the assets of the target company. An Asset Acquisition requires that each asset and liability acquired must be separately conveyed. For example, if a company sold all its assets, which primarily constituted land and buildings, separate legal documents would have to be prepared transferring each parcel of property. This requirement makes an Asset Acquisition more complicated than a Stock Acquisition, which merely requires the transfer of stock. Negotiations in an Asset Acquisition are conducted between the managements of the acquiring and target companies. Payment for the assets acquired is made to the target company. The target company remains in existence after the transaction, and stock ownership of the target company is unaffected. However, often the target company is liquidated after such a sale to place the proceeds of the sale in the hands of the target's stockholders.

2.402 Taxable versus Nontaxable Deals

Whether a deal is taxable or nontaxable depends on various Internal Revenue Code provisions. Certain basic concepts must be understood before one can address these complex provisions. The amount that a taxpayer realizes on the sale of any property is equal to the fair market value of all property received. The amount of gain or loss that a taxpayer "realizes" on the sale of property is computed by deducting the adjusted basis of the property sold from the amount realized.[3] As mentioned previously, a taxpayer's original basis in any property is equal to its cost, while the adjusted basis of the property at any point in time is equal to its original cost adjusted for certain items. Common adjustment items include depreciation, amortization, capital expenditures, earnings and profits, stock dividends, and distributions representing return of capital. The fact that a gain or loss is "realized" on a sale does not necessarily mean that the gain or loss will have current tax consequences. The gain or loss must be "recognized" to have current tax effects. The general rule under the present Tax Code is that all realized gains or losses will be recognized.[4] Acquisition transactions effected under this general rule are labeled **taxable transactions**. The Code also contains special provisions that defer the recognition of gain or loss until some future act triggers tax recognition of the gain or loss.[5] Transactions effected under these provisions are characterized as **nontaxable transactions**.

The theory behind deferring the recognition of gain or loss in tax-free transactions is that the shareholder is merely changing the form of his investment or exchanging stock in one company for stock in another. Both before and after the transaction, the stockholder has retained his investment in the business so the stockholder should not be taxed. This is why the tax-free acquisition provisions of the Code are called reorganization provisions. Philosophically, they involve reorganizations not acquisitions.

In order for a transaction to be a nontaxable reorganization, it must fit within one of the three types of reorganizations described in the Code. Each of these types of reorganizations has detailed requirements that are outlined in the next chapter. However, all reorganizations have certain general requirements that must also be met for a transaction to qualify as a tax-free reorganization. These general requirements were created judicially to deny tax-free status to transactions that do not come within the spirit of the reorganization provisions, although they satisfy the requirements of one of the tax-free provisions. There are four doctrines that make up the general requirements. They include the (*a*) Continuity of Interest Doctrine, (*b*) Continuity of Business Enterprise Doctrine, (*c*) Business Purpose Doctrine, and (*d*) Step Transaction Doctrine.[6]

Continuity of interest doctrine. The Continuity of Interest Doctrine requires that the shareholders of the target company obtain a continuing equity interest in the acquiring corporation. This has been interpreted to mean that a substantial portion of the consideration moving from the acquiring corporation be in the form of an equity interest in the acquiring corporation. Although the doctrine applies to all three types of reorganizations, the Continuity of Interest Doctrine has the most meaning in the context of a Type A Reorganization because there are specific statutory requirements covering the types of permissible consideration in the other two types of reorganizations. Based on case precedent, it appears that where the equity consideration paid by the acquiring corporation is less than 20 percent of the total consideration paid, tax-free treatment will probably be disallowed. Conversely, if the equity consideration is greater than 50 percent, there should be little problem with the Continuity of Interest Doctrine. In between 20–50 percent is the grey area where it is unclear how a particular case might be decided if it were to be fully litigated. The Continuity of Interest Doctrine must be applied within the framework of any pre-reorganization and post-reorganization transactions. If stock is sold by the target company's shareholders to the acquiring company or the target company redeems some of its stock prior to the tax-free reorganization, these transactions will generally be considered in determining whether the Continuity of Interest test has been met. If stockholders of the target dispose of the entire equity interest received from the acquiring company promptly after the tax-free reorganization, this would normally disqualify the tax-free nature of the transaction. A difficult question is how long the target company's shareholders must hold onto the equity interest received in order to preserve the tax-free nature of the transaction. The IRS would like to see a five-year holding period, although a shorter period should be sufficient, especially if there is a substantial change in the taxpayer's position.

Continuity of business enterprise doctrine. The Continuity of Business Enterprise Doctrine requires that the acquiring company must either (1) continue the target company's historic business or at least one significant line thereof or (2) use a significant portion of the target company's assets in its ongoing business. The target company's historic business is defined as the business it conducted immediately preceding the plan of reorganization. Basically, if the acquiring company sells the target company's assets and discontinues all of its lines of business, the Continuity of Business Enterprise test will not be met and the transaction will be a taxable event to the target company's shareholders.

Business purpose doctrine. The Business Purpose Doctrine requires that every reorganization must have a legitimate business purpose. Business purpose is defined as action that is required by business exigencies and that, by change in corporate form, reflects a continuing interest in property. This doctrine does not present any difficulties for transactions between unrelated parties.

Step transaction doctrine. The Step Transaction Doctrine requires the tax treatment of a transaction that is carried out in a series of steps follow the economic substance of the transaction rather than its form. For example, if a series of transactions entered into includes a tax-free reorganization, the transactions may be viewed as one taxable transaction. A number of factors come into play in determining whether a series of steps should be integrated including the time between transactions, intent of the parties, and the extent to which the transactions are linked.

NOTES TO CHAPTER 2

[1]IRC Section 1012.

[2]IRC Sections 1011 and 1016.

[3]IRC Section 1001.

[4]IRC Section 1001(c).

[5]IRC Section 368.

[6]See Boris I. Bittker and James S. Eustice, *Federal Income Taxation of Corporations and Shareholders,* 4th ed. (Boston, Mass.: Warren, Gorham & Lamont, 1979), par. 14.11 and 14.51 give a more detailed discussion of these doctrines.

Chapter 3

Alternate Acquisition Methods

3.1 INTRODUCTION

The concept that acquisitions are accomplished through one of six distinct acquisition methods was introduced in Chapter 1. In Chapter 2 the tax basis of the assets of the target company was identified as the key economic variable in most acquisitions, and the six acquisition methods were categorized according to how they handle this consideration. In this chapter we will examine in detail the six acquisition methods. The discussion of each method will include a general introduction followed by subsections analyzing the (1) treatment of acquirer—wherein the various tax consequences of the acquisition to the acquiring corporation will be discussed; and (2) treatment of target—wherein the tax consequences of the acquisition to the selling corporation or the selling shareholders will be reviewed. The accounting treatment for the various acquisition methods is reserved for Appendix C. However, it is important to note here that the accounting treatment of the various methods has no impact on an acquisition's economics.

3.2 NEW COST BASIS ACQUISITION METHODS

3.201 Asset Acquisition

3.201a In General
There are three types of Asset Acquisitions: (1) a straightforward Asset Acquisition, (2) a Statutory Merger, and (3) a Subsidiary Merger.

1. Asset Acquisition. In a straightforward Asset Acquisition the acquiring company purchases a part or all of the assets of the target company. The acquiring company pays cash or other consideration to the target company. Subsequent to the acquisition the target company remains in existence. However, often the target company liquidates to place the proceeds of the sale in the hands of the shareholders.[1]

EXAMPLE 3A *XYZ Corporation purchases all of the assets of ABC Corporation in an Asset Acquisition for $1,000. The target intends to take the proceeds from the sale and enter a new business.*

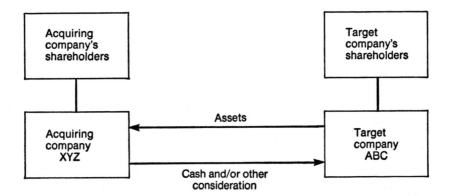

2. Statutory Merger. A Statutory Merger occurs when two or more corporations combine in such a way that one of the combining corporations remains in existence while the other participating corporations disappear. Statutory Mergers must be effected pursuant to a state statute. For tax purposes the target (merged) corporation is considered to have exchanged its assets for the consideration received such as cash notes, stock, etc. The target (merged) corporation is deemed liquidated and distributes the consideration received to its shareholders in exchange for their target (merged) corporation stock.

EXAMPLE 3B *Target ABC Corporation is merged into XYZ Corporation. ABC Corporation disappears by operation of law and XYZ Corporation survives. For tax purposes ABC is considered to have exchanged its assets for the consideration received (e.g., cash, notes, etc.) and distributed such consideration to its shareholders in exchange for their ABC stock.*

3. Subsidiary Merger. In a Subsidiary Merger the target company merges into a controlled subsidiary of the acquiring company in

Example 3B

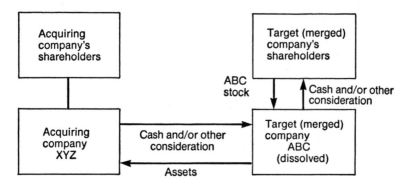

exchange for consideration (e.g., cash, notes, stock, etc.). For tax purposes the target (merged) corporation is considered to have exchanged its assets for the consideration received such as cash, notes, stock, etc. The target (merged) corporation is deemed liquidated and distributes the consideration received to its shareholders in exchange for their target (merged) corporation stock.

EXAMPLE 3C *Target ABC is merged into Sub Corporation, a wholly owned subsidiary of acquirer XYZ Corporation. ABC Corporation disappears by operation of law, and its shareholders receive consideration such as cash, notes, stock, etc. ABC is considered, for tax purposes, to have exchanged its assets for such consideration. ABC then distributes this consideration to its shareholders in exchange for their ABC stock.*

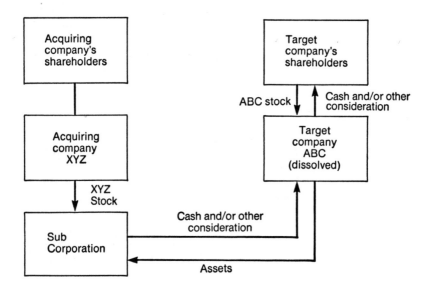

3.201b Treatment of Acquirer

In any Asset Acquisition there are four important areas to discuss relative to the acquiring corporation. These are the (1) tax basis of the assets acquired, (2) allocation of the purchase price, (3) the lack of carryover of tax attributes, and (4) investment tax credits available under this method.

1. Tax Basis of Assets Acquired. Under an Asset Acquisition method the acquiring corporation purchases a part or all of the assets of the target company for a price. This price is allocated among the assets acquired based on their fair market values.[2] The valuation of specific assets for tax purposes is discussed in paragraph 3.203d. The result is that each asset purchased ends up with a tax basis that is equal to its acquisition cost.

2. Allocation of the Purchase Price. How the total purchase price is allocated to the various assets in the contract in an Asset Acquisition is extremely important to the acquiring corporation and the target because it has direct economic consequences for both of them. The acquiring corporation is generally interested in assigning higher values to ordinary income items such as receivables, inventory, and depreciable assets. Moreover, within the depreciable asset categories the acquirer will want to assign greater values to assets with a 3-year or 5-year recovery period rather than to 10-year or 18-year property. The reason for the acquirer wanting such allocations is fairly obvious. Higher values assigned to ordinary income items will flow through the acquirer's income statement in a relatively short time and reduce taxable income. Higher values assigned to depreciable assets, especially assets with relatively short ACRS recovery periods, will also act to reduce the tax burden on the acquiring company. Moreover, the acquirer is extremely interested in keeping any allocation to goodwill kept at a minimum. The concept of goodwill is discussed in detail in paragraph 3.203c. The reason for this position is that the acquiring company will not be able to amortize the cost of this goodwill for tax purposes.

The target corporation usually takes a position diametrically opposed to that of the acquirer. The target generally wants a lower allocation of value to receivables and inventory because any gain associated with the sale of these assets will be taxed at ordinary income tax rates. The target also does not generally want high allocations to depreciable assets because the target will incur depreciation and investment tax credit recapture (see paragraphs B.405 and B.508). Finally, the target wants a high allocation to goodwill because goodwill is a capital asset. Therefore, any gain on the sale of goodwill will be taxed at capital gains rates.

The general rule for allocating the purchase price is fair market value. Where the acquirer and target arrive at an allocation of the purchase price when their interests are adverse, their allocation agreement will generally be respected by the IRS. However, if the parties interests are not adverse, as in the case where the target has adopted a plan of complete liquidation under Section 337 (described more fully later in paragraph 3.201c), the agreement is less likely to withstand an IRS challenge. A more detailed description of the mechanics of allocating the purchase price to various assets for tax purposes is contained in paragraph 3.203.

3. Lack of Carryover of Tax Attributes. In an Asset Acquisition there is no carryover of any tax attributes such as accounting method, earnings and profits account, capital loss carryovers, inventory methods, depreciation methods, and so forth. Thus, the acquiring company is not locked into any tax methods or characteristics of the target company. However, net operating losses, another tax attribute of the target company, are also not available to the acquiring company.

4. Investment Tax Credits Available. A minor amount ($12,500) of investment credits may be generated in an Asset Acquisition (see paragraph B.504). This limitation is brought about by the investment tax credit regulations regarding the purchase of used assets.

3.201c Treatment of Target

The target corporation in a straightforward Asset Acquisition remains in existence after the sale and is responsible for the tax due on any gain associated with the transaction. Basically, the target corporation is treated as if it had sold each asset individually.[3] Thus, the target must deal with the rules governing capital gains/losses, ordinary income, Section 1231 assets, depreciation, LIFO (last in, first out), and investment tax credit recapture to calculate its tax due on the sale. (See Appendix B for a review of these rules.)

The fact that the target corporation remains in existence after a straightforward Asset Acquisition is critical because in many transactions the shareholders of the target corporation are looking to wind up the business of the corporation. Generally, if the target corporation distributed the proceeds of the sale to its shareholders, the result would be that the corporation pays tax at the corporate level and the shareholder's would pay tax upon the distribution of the proceeds from the corporation. There are a number of tax planning techniques available to avoid this double taxation. However, the principle alternative is a liquidation of the corporation pursuant to Section 337 ("337 Liquidation"). Please note that in a Statutory Merger or Subsidiary Merger the merging corporation is automatically deemed liquidated. Under a **337 Liquidation,** no gain or loss is recognized by the target corporation if the corporation adopts a plan of complete liquidation and distributes all of its assets pursuant to that plan. The sale of its assets and the distribution in liquidation must both take place within the same 12-month period, beginning upon the date the plan of complete liquidation is adopted. There are a few exceptions to the general nonrecognition of gain or loss rule of Section 337, the most important of which is that the target corporation must still recognize as ordinary income depreciation and investment tax credits recaptured as a result of the sale[4] (see paragraphs B.405 and B.508) and the LIFO recapture amount (see paragraph B.7). The net effect of the rules under 337 is to put shareholders of the target corporation in roughly the same position as if they had sold their stock in a 338 Transaction. Usually the only significant difference between the two methods, as between the acquiring company and the target company's shareholders, is that the target company (and therefore the target company's shareholders) pays any tax on recapture income in an Asset Acquisition whereas the acquiring company ultimately bears the burden of the tax in a 338 Transaction.

3.202   338 Transaction

3.202a   In General

A 338 Transaction occurs if the acquiring corporation purchases within a 12-month period at least 80 percent of the voting shares and at least 80 percent of all other stock (other than nonvoting preferred) of the target and elects within approximately nine months after it has purchased the stock to treat the transaction as if the target company sold its assets on the acquisition date to a new corporation for a price equal to the stock acquisition price.[5] In this transaction the target company is considered to have sold its assets at their fair market value while the acquiring company is deemed to have purchased the assets of the target for an amount equal to the price paid for the targets stock (assuming all stock held was purchased within the previous 12 months). In this type of transaction the acquiring company buys the stock of the target company from its shareholders. In situations where the target company is a wholly owned subsidiary of a larger corporation, the sole stockholder is the parent company. The effect of the transaction is that the target becomes a subsidiary of the acquiring company.

EXAMPLE 3D *XYZ Corporation purchases all of the outstanding stock of ABC Corporation in a 338 Transaction. XYZ Corporation makes the necessary tax election.*

Example 3D

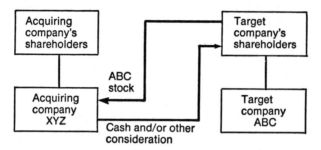

3.202b Treatment of Acquirer

The discussion of how a 338 Transaction affects the acquiring corporation is broken down into eight segments: (1) selling price to target company, (2) deemed purchase price determination, (3) tax basis of assets acquired, (4) allocation of the purchase price, (5) recognition of gain or loss on the asset sale, (6) who pays the target company's tax, (7) lack of carryover of tax attributes and (8) effect of liquidation of target.

1. Selling Price to Target Company.   The target company is considered to have sold its assets to the new corporation at their fair market value. Fair market value may be determined on the basis of an elective formula to be provided in regulations which have not yet been issued or on the basis of a proper appraisal.

2. Deemed Purchase Price Determination.   Generally the new corporation is deemed to have purchased the assets of the target for an amount equal to the price paid for the target's stock adjusted for liabilities assumed. However special rules for determining the purchase price exist if the acquiring company did not purchase all of the target's stock within the 12-month acquisition period.

3. Tax Basis of Assets Acquired.   The new corporation takes a basis in the assets acquired equal to the deemed purchase price. Assuming 100 percent of the target's stock has been purchased within the last 12 months, the new corporation takes a basis in the target's assets equal to the cost of the target corporation's stock plus an amount equal to the total depreciation, investment tax credit, LIFO recapture, and all other recapture tax liability.[6]

4. Allocation of Purchase Price.   The basis described above is allocated to individual assets pursuant to regulations which will be issued under Section 338(b) (3). For purposes of this book it is reasonable to assume that these regulations will not be materially different from the allocation method used in an Asset Acquisition (see paragraph 3.203).

5. Recognition of Gain/Loss on Asset Sale. If the acquiring company makes a proper election under Section 338, then for tax purposes the target company is "deemed" to have "sold all of its assets at the close of the acquisition date in a single transaction to which Section 337 applies." Section 337 as described previously affords a target corporation nonrecognition of gain or loss treatment if the corporation adopts a plan of complete liquidation and distributes all of its assets pursuant to that plan. Thus, the target company will not generally recognize gain or loss on the sale. However, the LIFO, investment credit, and depreciation recapture rules override Section 337.[7]

6. Who Pays the Target Company's Tax? If the target company has income on the deemed sale pursuant to the LIFO, investment credit, or depreciation recapture provisions, who pays the tax? The target pays the tax liability arising from the deemed sale, but the acquiring company actually bears the economic burden. How? In situations where the target's results are included in a parent seller's consolidated tax return up until the acquisition date, the target must file a separate final tax return to report the tax liability arising from the deemed sale of assets.[8] This tax return (called deemed sale return) only includes items from the deemed sale, except for certain miscellaneous carryover items from the consolidated return of the selling group. The tax liability from the deemed sale cannot be included in the selling parent corporation's consolidated return because the target is presumed disaffiliated from the selling group immediately before the deemed sale. Furthermore, the deemed sale cannot be reported in the consolidated return of the acquiring corporation. The net effect of these rules is to place responsibility for payment of any tax liability on the target. Since this liability must be paid out of the target's assets, it diminishes the net assets available to the acquiring corporation. In instances where the target is not part of a consolidated group prior to the transaction, the target still files a final tax return that includes the deemed sale. The acquiring company bears the economic burden here again because the transaction has the effect of reducing the net assets of the target that are available to the acquiring company.

It is important to remember that since the target recognizes income on the deemed sale, the new corporation will receive an upward basis adjustment for its assets equal to the tax associated with the depreciation, LIFO, and investment tax credits recaptured.

7. Lack of Carryover of Tax Attributes. Under preexisting law a corporation that purchased the stock of another corporation did not succeed to any tax attributes (e.g., net operating loss carryforwards) of the target corporation upon liquidation. Similarly, under Section 338 there is no carryover of tax attributes.

8. Effect of Liquidation of Target. Generally, the liquidation of the target company on or after the acquisition date has very little effect. Liquidation on the acquisition date is considered to occur on the following day and after the deemed sale. The liquidation is treated as tax-free to both the target and acquiring corporations, and the acquiring corporation takes over the target company's basis in its assets and other tax attributes.[9]

3.202c   Treatment of Target

Generally, the tax considerations for the target's shareholders in a 338 Transaction are straightforward. The stock that is sold is generally a capital asset in the hands of the stockholders. On its sale the stockholders recognize a capital gain or loss that is equal to the difference between the amount realized and the stockholders' basis in the stock (see paragraph B.302). However, if part of the consideration received by the target's shareholders is for an employment or consulting contract or a covenant not to compete some portion of the purchase price might be allocated to that item, in which case the shareholder would recognize ordinary income. An important feature of a stock sale is that generally the shareholders avoid the problem of recapture that is associated with an Asset Acquisition.

3.203   Allocating the Purchase Price for Tax Purposes

3.203a   Basic Rule

In both New Cost Basis Acquisition Methods—(1) an Asset Acquisition and (2) a 338 Transaction—the allocation of the purchase price to the target company's assets is an extremely important consideration. This paragraph is devoted to reviewing the mechanics of this allocation process.

The basic rule for allocating the purchase price to the assets purchased is to allocate the aggregate basis (purchase cost) to the assets in relation to their fair market values. The fair market valuation of specific assets for tax purposes is discussed in paragraph 3.203d. Purchase price is defined herein as the price paid for the assets or stock plus certain adjustments such as liabilities assumed, recapture tax, and so forth. Although the above sounds like a straightforward rule, it is difficult to apply in practice because it requires determining the value of each asset. As the starting point in an Asset Acquisition, the lump-sum price is allocated first to cash, marketable securities, prepaid expenses, receivables, and inventory to the extent of their respective fair market values with the remainder being allocated among other assets on the basis of their relative fair market values. If the total market value of all the assets equals the purchase price, then the allocation process is complete. If, however, there is any difference, plus or minus, between the sum of the "appraised" fair market values of the assets including goodwill and the purchase price, then a second tier adjustment is required to arrive at the new tax basis of the assets of the target. If the purchase price exceeds the sum of the appraised fair market values of the assets of the target, there has been a premium purchase; whereas if the purchase price is less than the sum of the appraised fair market values of the target's assets, there has been a bargain purchase. The second tier allocation for each asset category is computed by dividing the asset categories' appraised fair market value by the total appraised fair market values of the asset categories to be included in the second tier allocation. The resulting fraction for each asset category is then multiplied by the difference between the purchase price and the total appraised fair market values of the assets to determine the second tier allocation for each asset category. The second tier allocations are added to or subtracted from the appraised fair market values of the asset categories to find the new tax basis of the target's assets. For second tier allocation purposes, receivables cannot be stepped up above their gross value. Furthermore, cash is unaffected by any second tier allocation.

EXAMPLE 3E *ABC Corporation sells all of its assets to XYZ in an Asset Acquisition for $1,000. ABC's assets and their respective fair market values are listed below. What is their new tax basis in the hands of XYZ?*

Asset	(A) Fair Market Value	(B) Second Tier Allocation Calculation	(C) Allocation	(A) and (C) Tax Basis
Cash	$ 30			$ 30
Receivables	140*			140
Inventories	280	($280/$630) × ($1,000 − $800) = $89		369
Property, plant and equipment	170	($170/$630) × ($1,000 − $800) =	54	224
Goodwill	180	($180/$630) × ($1,000 − $800) =	57	237
	$800			$1,000

*Equals gross value.

EXAMPLE 3F *Same as Example 3E except the purchase price is $500.*

Asset	(A) Fair Market Value	(B) Second Tier Allocation Calculation	(C) Allocation	(A) and (C) Tax Basis
Cash	$ 30			$ 30
Receivables	140			140
Inventories	280	($280/$630) × ($500 − $800) = ($133)		147
Property, plant and equipment	170	($170/$630) × ($500 − $800) =	(81)	89
Goodwill	180	($180/$630) × ($500 − $800) =	(86)	94
	$800			$500

In a 338 Transaction the IRS has been authorized to issue regulations prescribing the approach to take in allocating the purchase price to the assets of the target company. Any difference between these regulations and the approach taken above will in most cases not be material for purposes of valuing a business using the methods described in this book.

3.203b Substantiating the Allocation

In an Asset Acquisition the parties often attempt to substantiate their allocation of the purchase price by including it in the purchase contract. If the allocation was arrived at in arm's-length negotiations by parties with adverse interests, the allocation will usually be accepted. However, in an Asset Acquisition where there is no such allocation in the contract or in a 338 Transaction, the acquiring company usually attempts to substantiate its allocation by obtaining independent appraisals of the assets acquired.

3.203c Goodwill

Goodwill for tax purposes is generally defined as an expectancy of earnings in excess of a normal return on the assets employed in a business. This expectancy of excess returns can come from any number of factors including location, trade secrets, brand names, reputation, or management skill. Whether or not goodwill exists in an acquisition is determined using the valuation methods described below. When goodwill is found to exist, the acquiring company pays for an asset for which it cannot receive a tax deduction. The situation is particularly troublesome as indicated below for management of the acquiring company because for financial accounting purposes it must amortize any goodwill over a period not to exceed 40 years.

In order to fully understand the nature of goodwill we will compare the accounting and tax consequences where $1,000 of purchase price is allocated to goodwill. For book purposes we will amortize goodwill over 40 years on a straight-line basis. As mentioned, goodwill cannot be amortized for tax purposes. The book figures in the table represent the effect on the company's operating profit before taxes for financial statement purposes and the tax figures represent the effect on

Goodwill

Year	Book	Tax
1	$(25)	—
2	(25)	—
3	(25)	—
4	(25)	—
5	(25)	—

the company's taxable income. If the purchase price is allocated to goodwill, the acquiring company must deduct $25 annually from its book profit while it receives no deduction from taxable income.

3.203d Valuing Specific Assets

The purchase price can be thought of as having two components: a working capital component and the remainder. The remainder consists of the value paid for net property, plant, and equipment; intangible assets; and goodwill. Following is a review of how each asset is valued within each of these groups, and some associated tax problems.

Working Capital Assets
Cash—valued dollar for dollar.

Marketable Securities—generally have a readily determinable value and are usually capital assets in the hands of the target.

Receivables—normally valued on a dollar for dollar basis and are not capital assets.

Inventory—usually valued at net realizable value that is the estimated sales price less the cost of disposition and a reasonable allowance for profit.[10] Given that there are no regulations defining reasonable profit, this is an area where practice varies widely. Inventory is not a capital asset in the hands of the seller, and thus any gain associated with its sale will be taxed at ordinary rates.

Prepaid Expenses—usually valued on a dollar for dollar basis. However, if prepaid expenses cover extensive periods going forward, the amounts may be discounted.

Remainder
Property, Plant, and Equipment—Property, plant, and equipment used in a business are Section 1231 assets in the hands of the target. Thus, the target is afforded favorable tax treatment on their disposition, assuming the assets have been held longer than one year (see paragraph B.303). These assets are generally valued for tax purposes by having appraisals done. These appraisals take into account the particular assets: their condition, location, profit generating potential; market prices for similar assets; replacement cost; and other relevant factors.

Intangible Assets—The acquiring company is not limited to allocating the purchase price to assets appearing on the seller's books. Thus, the acquiring company may be able to allocate substantial value to certain intangible assets such as patents, copyrights, contract rights, and leases that the acquiring company can then amortize over the useful life of the particular asset. This option is important when the value that is attributed to these intangibles would otherwise be allocated to goodwill. The target corporation will generally favor an allocation to these assets because these assets are usually capital assets.

Goodwill—The IRS values goodwill using one of three approaches and generally argues for the method that results in the largest amount of goodwill. First, is the residual value method (also called the subtraction or gap method). In this approach all assets other then goodwill are valued and their total is subtracted from the purchase price. To the extent some value remains, this is goodwill.[11] Another approach is to calculate goodwill using a formula.[12] This formula involves capitalizing the earnings stream of the target that exceeds a fair rate of return on the net tangible assets of the company. A fair rate of return is the rate of return prevailing in the industry on the sale date. If such a figure is unavailable, the IRS generally uses 8–10 percent. The capitalization rate used is 15 percent if the business has stable earnings and low risk and 20 percent if the business has high risk.

EXAMPLE 3G   *ABC Corporation has net tangible assets for the last five years as follows:*

1980	$1,426
1981	1,947
1982	1,862
1983	1,765
1984	2,104
Total	9,103
	÷5
Average net tangible assets	1,821
Fair rate of return (8–10%), say	10%
	182
Capitalization rate (15–20%), say, 20%	
$\dfrac{1.00}{.20} = 5$ multiple	× 5
	$ 910

If ABC Corporation was sold for $1,000, the formula method would indicate that goodwill of $90 ($1,000 − $910) existed.

The final approach that the IRS uses is going-concern value. Under this approach the IRS argues that although goodwill may not be present, another nonamortizable intangible asset "going-concern value" is. Going-concern value is the value associated with purchasing an up and running business. The IRS attempts to quantify going-concern value by estimating the start-up losses that one would incur to build such a business and present value these losses. This approach is highly controversial.

3.203e Special Allocations

There are certain situations in which the acquirer can allocate some of the value to be given to the target company to items that will result in current deductions. These include a covenant not to compete and employment or consulting contracts. If a covenant not to compete is agreed to in the purchase contract and value is assigned to it, the acquiring company can amortize the cost of that covenant during its useful life. The usefulness of the employment or consulting contract is self-evident. In both cases the target will receive ordinary income and the acquirer will obtain an ordinary deduction.

3.3   NO CHANGE IN BASIS ACQUISITION METHODS

3.301   Stock Acquisition

3.301a   In General

There are three types of Stock Acquisitions: (1) a straightforward Stock Acquisition, (2) a Reverse Statutory Merger, and (3) a Reverse Subsidiary Merger.

1. Stock Acquisition. A straightforward Stock Acquisition occurs when the acquiring company purchases the stock of the target company from its shareholders and does nothing else.

EXAMPLE 3H *XYZ Corporation acquires all of the stock of ABC Corporation in a Stock Acquisition.*

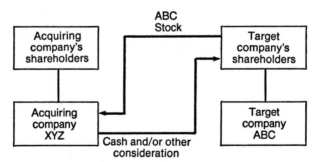

2. Reverse Statutory Merger. A Reverse Statutory Merger is merely a Statutory Merger accomplished in such a manner that the acquiring company merges into the target company. For tax purposes the transaction is treated as a sale and purchase of stock with the acquiring corporation deemed merged downstream into the target.

EXAMPLE 3I *Acquiring company XYZ Corporation merges into target ABC Corporation. XYZ Corporation disappears by operation of law, and ABC Corporation survives. For tax purposes XYZ Corporation is considered to have purchased the stock of ABC Corporation.*

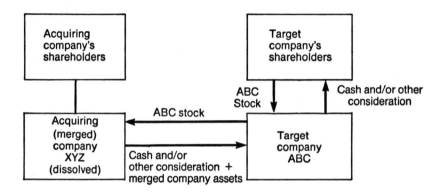

3. Reverse Subsidiary Merger. In a Reverse Subsidiary Merger a controlled subsidiary of the acquiring company merges into the target company. The primary reason that these types of transactions are done is that there is some legal need to maintain the target corporation's existence. The target company's shareholders receive cash, notes, stock, or other consideration, and the acquiring company receives the stock of the target company. For tax purposes the transaction is viewed as a sale of stock by the target company's shareholders.

EXAMPLE 3J *Sub Corporation, a wholly owned subsidiary of XYZ Corporation, merges into ABC Corporation, the target company. Sub Corporation disappears by operation of law. The target company's shareholders receive cash, notes, stock, or other consideration in exchange for their target company stock.*

3.301b Treatment of Acquirer

The tax treatment of the acquiring company in a Stock Acquisition is fairly simple. The acquiring company takes a basis in the stock of the target company equal to its cost, and the tax attributes of the target company (e.g., accounting method, tax basis of its assets, net operating losses, etc.) are unaffected by the change in ownership. One major exception exists to the general rule regarding carryover of tax attributes. If the acquiring company (technically the top 10 shareholders) *(a)* acquires 50 percent or more of the stock of the target company either through a purchase from another unrelated party or through a decrease of the number of shares outstanding over a period dating back approxi-

Example 3J

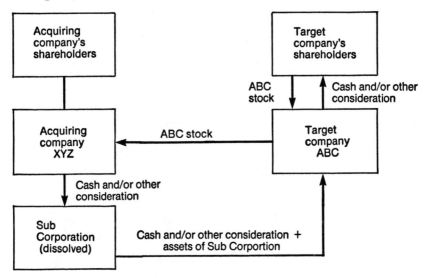

mately two years, and *(b)* the company does not substantially carry on the same trade or business, then any net operating loss carried forward will not be allowed.[13] Moreover, even if the losses are allowed, they generally can only be used against the target's own future income and not against the income of a group that it files a consolidated return with after the date of acquisition.

3.301c Treatment of Target
The tax treatment of the target's shareholders in this type of acquisition is substantially similar to the tax treatment of the selling shareholders in a 338 Transaction. The stock that is sold is generally a capital asset in the hands of the stockholders. On its sale the stockholders recognize a capital gain or loss that is equal to the difference between the amount realized and the stockholder's basis in the stock. However, if part of the consideration received by the selling shareholders was for an employment or consulting contract or a covenant not to compete some portion of the purchase price might be allocated to that item, in which case the selling shareholder would recognize ordinary income.

3.302 Type A Reorganization

3.302a In General
Transactions that are effected as a Type A Reorganization come in four different forms: (1) Type A Statutory Merger,[14] (2) Type A Statutory Consolidation,[15] (3) Type A Subsidiary Merger,[16] and (4) Type A Re-

verse Subsidiary Merger.[17] As a general rule the acquiring company can use voting or nonvoting common stock, or voting or nonvoting preferred stock, or a combination thereof to effect a nontaxable merger. However, in a Type A Reverse Subsidiary Merger the stockholders of the target corporation must receive only voting stock of the acquiring corporation in exchange for control of the target.[18] Control is defined to be at least 80 percent of all the outstanding voting stock and 80 percent of the total number of shares of each of the other outstanding classes of stock of the target. The acquiring company can also use a substantial amount of cash, debt instruments, warrants, or options (boot) in a tax-free merger subject to the Continuity of Interest Doctrine. Based on case precedent on this doctrine, it appears that where the equity consideration paid by the acquiring corporation is less than 20 percent of the total consideration paid, tax-free treatment will probably be disallowed. Conversely, if the equity consideration is greater than 50 percent, there should be little problem with the Continuity of Interest Doctrine. In between 20–50 percent is the grey area where it is unclear how a particular case might be decided if it were to be fully litigated. However, note that due to the voting stock requirement in a Type A Reverse Subsidiary Merger, the use of boot in such a transaction is limited to 20 percent of the consideration paid.

The ability to use boot in a Type A Reorganization makes this acquisition method extremely popular. One frequently used approach in the tax-free merger area is a Cash Option Merger. In a **Cash Option Merger** the acquiring company grants an option to the target company's shareholders to accept either cash or its stock in exchange for their target company stock. The purpose in granting such an option is to afford tax-free results to those shareholders who desire it and taxable results to those who want cash. In fulfilling the Continuity of Interest requirements in this context, it is important to remember that only one or more shareholders of the target need receive the requisite proprietary interest in the acquiring company. Pro rata receipt of the acquiring company's stock is unnecessary. A typical situation where a Cash Option Merger would be used is when the target is owned primarily (say, 40–60 percent) by one person or family with the rest of the common stock owned by the public. The principal shareholders may want an ownership interest in the acquiring company as well as tax-free treatment. The acquiring company would offer a package of cash and stock to the target's shareholders with the public taking the cash and the controlling shareholders the stock.

1. Type A Statutory Merger. A Type A Statutory Merger occurs when two or more corporations combine in such a way that one of the combining corporations remains in existence while the other participating corporations disappear. Statutory mergers must be effected pursuant to a state statute. For tax purposes the target (merged) corporation is considered to have exchanged its assets for the stock of the acquiring (surviving) corporation. The target (merged) corporation distributes the stock of the acquiring corporation to its shareholders in exchange for their target (merged) corporation stock.

EXAMPLE 3K *Target ABC Corporation is merged into XYZ Corporation. ABC Corporation disappears by operation of law and XYZ Corporation survives. For tax purposes ABC is considered to have exchanged its assets for XYZ stock and distributed the XYZ stock to its shareholders in exchange for their ABC stock.*

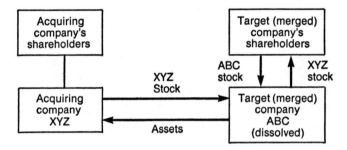

2. Type A Statutory Consolidation.

A Type A Statutory Consolidation is effected when two or more corporations are combined into a new corporation. The new corporation sometimes comes into existence by operation of law and sometimes it must be formed. Which rule is applicable depends on state law. For tax purposes the combined corporations are considered to have exchanged their assets for the stock of the new corporation. Upon receiving the stock of the new corporation, the combined corporations distribute it to their shareholders in exchange for their stock in the combined corporation.

EXAMPLE 3L *Target ABC Corporation and acquirer XYZ Corporation are combined in a Type A Statutory Consolidation. Both ABC and XYZ disappear and an entirely new corporation (NewCo) results. For tax purposes ABC Corporation and XYZ Corporation are considered to have exchanged their assets for the stock of the new corporation. ABC and XYZ distribute this stock to their shareholders in exchange for their stock.*

Example 3L

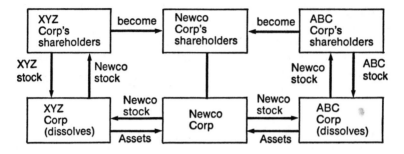

3. Type A Subsidiary Merger. In a Type A Subsidiary Merger (also called **Standard Triangular Merger**) the target company merges into a controlled subsidiary of the acquiring company in exchange for the stock of the acquiring company.[19] The acquiring company must acquire substantially all of the assets of the target company, and no stock of the subsidiary can be given as consideration to the shareholders of the target company. In order to receive an advance ruling from the IRS indicating the transaction will qualify as a reorganization, the acquiring company must meet the IRS definition of "substantially all" which is at least 90 percent of the fair market value of the target's net assets and at least 70 percent of the fair market value of the target's gross assets immediately preceding the transaction.[20]

As with a Type A Statutory Merger the target (merged) corporation is considered, for tax purposes, to have exchanged its assets for stock. The target (merged) corporation distributes the stock received to its shareholders in exchange for their company stock.

EXAMPLE 3M   *Target ABC is merged into Sub Corporation, a wholly owned subsidiary of acquirer XYZ Corporation. ABC Corporation disappears by operation of law, and its shareholders receive stock of XYZ Corporation. ABC is considered, for tax purposes, to have exchanged its assets for XYZ stock. ABC then distributed the XYZ stock to its shareholders in exchange for their ABC stock.*

4. Type A Reverse Subsidiary Merger. In a Type A Reverse Subsidiary Merger a controlled subsidiary of the acquiring company merges into the target company. The primary reason that these types of transactions are done is that there is some legal need to maintain the target corporation's existence. The target company's shareholders receive stock of the acquiring company and the acquiring company receives the stock of the target company. The merger agreement usually provides that when the merger takes place the shares of the subsidiary

Example 3M

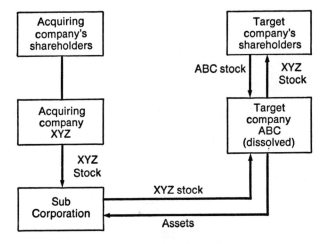

automatically become shares of the target company. The net effect is that the target company survives the transaction and becomes a subsidiary of the acquiring company. After the transaction the target company must hold substantially all (as previously defined) of the assets it held before the transaction as well as substantially all the assets of the subsidiary (excluding stock or cash dropped down from the acquiring company to effect the transaction) that merged into it.[21]

EXAMPLE 3N *Sub Corporation, a wholly owned subsidiary of XYZ Corporation, merges into ABC Corporation, the target company. Sub Corporation disappears by operation of law. The target company's shareholders receive stock of XYZ in exchange for their stock in ABC.*

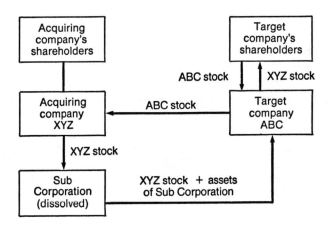

After the transaction the target is a subsidiary of the acquiring company:

Example 3N

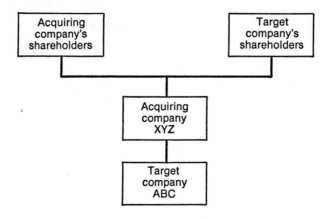

3.302b   Treatment of Acquirer

The acquiring company or its subsidiary does not recognize any gain or loss in any Type A Reorganization[22] and takes a carryover basis in the assets of the target company.[23] It is the rule rather than the exception that boot is paid in this method of acquisition. Yet, the use of boot and any recognition of gain by the shareholders of the target does not effect the basis of the target company's assets in the hands of the acquiring company or its subsidiary.[24] The target company's net operating losses are carried over in this type of acquisition[25] (but see discussion in paragraph B.8 on limitations applicable to these losses).

3.302c   Treatment of Target

In general, a Type A Reorganization is tax free to both the target company and its shareholders.[26] The shareholders take a basis in the stock received that is the same as for the stock they surrendered.[27] If a stockholder receives boot, the stockholder will recognize taxable gain.[28] If the receipt of boot has the effect of a distribution of a dividend, it will be taxed as such.[29] If not, the boot will be taxed as gain on the sale of a capital asset. Assuming the stock exchanged was held for the requisite period, the gain will be taxed at capital gains rates. In any event where there is boot the stockholder's basis in any stock received will be decreased for the amount of the boot and increased for the amount of the gain recognized.[30]

3.303   Type B Reorganization

3.303a   In General

A Type B Reorganization is generally accomplished in two ways: (1) Parent Stock for Stock Exchange between the acquiring company and the target's shareholders and (2) Subsidiary Stock for Stock Exchange between a subsidiary of the acquiring company and the target's shareholders.[31] In either transaction the only consideration that can be used by the acquiring company is voting stock. Voting stock is generally defined as any class of stock that has a right to vote for directors and therefore includes voting preferred stock. Any consideration, no matter how small, other than voting stock will destroy the transactions status as a Type B Reorganization. However, the target corporation can make ordinary dividend distributions or redeem shares prior to the reorganization without affecting its tax-free status.[32] In any redemption, care must be taken not to run afoul of the Continuity of Interest requirement (see paragraph 2.402).

1. Parent Stock for Stock Exchange. In this transaction the acquiring company exchanges its voting stock for stock of the target company. After the transaction the acquiring company must have control of the target. Control is defined as ownership of stock possessing at least 80 percent of the total combined voting power of all classes of stock entitled to vote and at least 80 percent of the total number of shares of all other classes of stock of the target. The effect of the transaction is that the target company becomes a subsidiary of the acquiring company.

EXAMPLE 30   *XYZ Corporation agrees to buy ABC Corporation in a Parent Stock for Stock Exchange. XYZ issues its stock to ABC Corporation in exchange for ABC stock.*

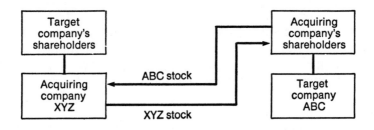

2. Subsidiary Stock for Stock Exchange. In a Subsidiary Stock for Stock Transaction the acquiring company can only use its own stock or that of its subsidiary as consideration. A combination of the two is not allowed. The mechanics work basically the same as above except that the acquiring company contributes its stock down to the subsidiary (assuming the acquiring company's stock is the consideration to be used) which then exchanges that stock for the stock of the target. As above, the subsidiary must have control of the target after the transaction. The use of a subsidiary to effect the transaction makes the target a subsidiary of the acquiring company's subsidiary.

EXAMPLE 3P *XYZ Corporation agrees to buy ABC Corporation in a Subsidiary Stock for Stock Exchange. XYZ contributes its stock down to its wholly owned subsidiary, Sub Corporation, which then exchanges this stock for the target company's stock.*

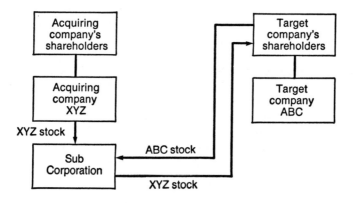

3.303b   Treatment of Acquirer

The acquiring company or its subsidiary does not recognize any gain or loss in a Type B Reorganization[33] and takes a carryover basis in the assets of the target company.[34] In a Subsidiary Stock for Stock Transaction the acquiring company takes a basis in the stock of its original subsidiary equal to the basis of the stock of the target's shareholders.[35] Any net operating losses of the target are also carried over subject to the limitations described in paragraph B.8.[36]

3.303c   Treatment of Target

The transaction has no effect on the target company whatsoever. Moreover, the target company shareholders do not recognize any gain or loss in the transaction[37] and take a basis in the stock received equal to their basis in the stock of the target company.[38]

3.304 Type C Reorganization

3.304a In General

A Type C Reorganization can be effected in two ways: (1) Parent Stock for Assets Transaction between the acquiring company and the target company and (2) Subsidiary Stock for Assets Transaction between a subsidiary of the acquiring company and the target company.[39] In these transactions the acquiring company or its subsidiary purchases substantially all of the assets of the target (subject to all or part of its liabilities) in exchange for voting stock (common or preferred) of either (but not both) the acquiring company or its subsidiary. Substantially all of the properties of the target is generally taken to mean 90 percent of the net assets of the target company.[40] However, a lower percentage can be adequate in certain circumstances based on the nature of the properties retained, the reason for retaining them and their amount. The key seems to be that the operating assets of the target company must be conveyed. Due to the restrictive nature of the consideration that may be given in these transactions, the target company would ordinarily look to alternatives such as redemptions or spin-offs to mitigate these restrictions. Unfortunately, the Step Transaction Doctrine and the "substantially all" requirements block the use of such techniques. However, normal dividends do not cause problems with these rules.

In certain limited instances the acquiring company can give as consideration cash and other property (boot) rather than voting stock. Boot may be given to the extent that the liabilities assumed by the acquiring company or its subsidiary are less than 20 percent of the gross value of the assets conveyed.[41]

The assumption by the acquiring company or its subsidiary of the target's liabilities does not affect the tax-free nature of the transaction unless the liabilities constitute a disproportionately large percentage of the fair market value of the target's assets. In such event the transaction may be treated as a taxable sale.

The target must distribute the stock, securities, and other consideration received in the reorganization as well as its other assets for the transaction to qualify as a Type C Reorganization.

1. Parent Stock for Assets Transaction. This transaction consists of the acquiring company exchanging its voting stock for substantially all of the assets of the target company.

EXAMPLE 3Q *XYZ Corporation agrees to purchase all ABC Corporation's assets and liabilities in a Parent Stock for Assets Transaction. XYZ Corporation exchanges its voting stock for substantially all of the assets of ABC Corpo-*

ration. ABC Corporation distributes all of its assets including the XYZ stock to its shareholders.

Example 3Q

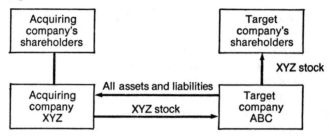

2. Subsidiary Stock for Assets Transaction. In this transaction the subsidiary of the acquiring company exchanges its voting stock or the voting stock of the acquiring company for substantially all of the assets of the target company.

EXAMPLE 3R *XYZ Corporation agrees to purchase all ABC Corporation's assets and liabilities in a Subsidiary Stock for Assets Transaction. Sub Corporation, a wholly owned subsidiary of XYZ Corporation, exchanges the voting stock of XYZ Corporation for substantially all of the assets of ABC Corporation. ABC Corporation distributes all of its assets including the XYZ stock to its shareholders.*

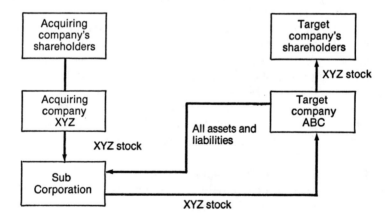

3.304b   *Treatment of Acquirer*

The acquiring company or its subsidiary does not generally recognize any gain or loss in a Type C Reorganization[42] and takes a carryover basis in the assets acquired.[43] If boot is given to the target company and distributed by the target to its shareholders, their recognition of gain will not affect the basis of the target company's assets in the hands of the acquiring company.[44]

3.304c   Treatment of Target

The target company and its shareholders do not recognize any gain or loss if only voting stock of the acquiring company or its subsidiary is received by the target company for its assets and distributed to its shareholders. When the target company is liquidated, the shareholders will take a basis in the acquiring company's stock equal to the basis in their target company stock. In the event that boot is used in the transaction and distributed to the target company's shareholders, it is taxable to the shareholders.

NOTES TO CHAPTER 3

[1]See IRC Section 337.

[2]Rev. Rul. 55–79, 1955–1 C.B. 370.

[3]Ibid.

[4]IRC Sections 47(a), 1245, 1250.

[5]IRC Section 338.

[6]James S. Eustice, *Federal Income Taxation of Corporations and Shareholders 1983 Cumulative Supplement No. 3* (Boston, Mass: Warren, Gorham & Lamont, 1983), par. 11.47.

[7]IRC Sections 47(a), 1245, 1250.

[8]See Prop. Regs. 1.338.

[9]IRC Sections 336, 332, 334(b)(1).

[10]Rev. Proc. 77–12, 1977–1 C.B. 569.

[11]*R. M. Smith, Inc.* v. *Commissioner 69 T. C.*

[12]Rev. Rul. 68–609, 1968–2 C. B. 327.

[13]IRC Section 382(a).

[14]IRC Section 368(a)(1)(A).

[15]IRC Section 368(a)(1)(A).

[16]IRC Section 368(a)(2)(D).

[17]IRC Section 368(a)(2)(E).

[18]IRC Section 368(a)(2)(E).

[19]IRC Section 368(a)(2)(D).

[20]Rev. Proc. 77–37, 1977–2 C. B. 568.

[21]IRC Section368(a)(2)(E).

[22]IRC Section 1032 indicates that a corporation issuing its own stock to purchase assets does not recognize any gain or loss.

[23]IRC Section 362(b). Note also that in a Reverse Subsidiary Merger the acquiring company's basis in its stock in the target is equal to the target's net asset basis. See Prop. Regs. 1.358–6(c).

[24]However, if boot is paid to the target corporation but not distributed to the target's shareholders, Section 362(b) provides that the basis of the target company's assets will be increased by the gain recognized by the target company under Section 361(b)(1)(B).

[25]IRC Section 381.

[26]IRC Section 354(a)(1).

[27]IRC Section 358(a).

[28]IRC Section 356.

[29]IRC Section 356(a)(2).

[30]IRC Section 358(a).

[31]IRC Section 368(a)(1)(B).

[32]Rev. Rul 75–360, 1975–2 C. B. 110.

[33]IRC Section 1032.

[34]IRC Section 362(b).

[35]Prop. Reg. 1.358–6(a) and 1.358–6(b).

[36]IRC Section 381.

[37]IRC Section 354(a)(1).

[38]IRC Section 358(a)(1).

[39]IRC Section 368(a)(1)(C).

[40]Rev. Proc. 77–37, 1977–2 C. B. 568.

[41]IRC Section 368(a)(2)(B).

[42]Section 1032.

[43]Section 362(b).

[44]Section 362(b).

Chapter 4

Theoretical Framework

4.1 INTRODUCTION

The buyer and seller in any purchase transaction generally have diametrically opposed economic interests. Simply put, the buyer is looking to negotiate a deal at the lowest cost whereas the seller wants to maximize the sale price. These basic economic rules are difficult to apply in the context of acquiring a business because of tax law complications. The purpose of this chapter is to outline a theoretical framework for calculating the real economic cost and proceeds in a transaction as well as review the nontax factors that influence the buyer and seller.

4.2 BUYER'S PERSPECTIVE

4.201 Net Present Tax Cost (NPTC)

Appendix A reviews the discounted cash flow techniques that will be used to analyze acquisitions. One of those techniques involves finding the net present value of a project. This concept will be modified slightly to allow us to determine the true economic cost of an acquisition. Remember we are only discussing costs in this section. Therefore, operating cash flows do not enter into our analysis here. This cost will hereafter be referred to as the Net Present Tax Cost or NPTC. The **NPTC** will be defined as being equal to the present cash outflow associated with the acquisition less the present value of the future tax benefits that arise due to the fact that certain of the target company's assets can be depreciated or amortized for tax purposes. All other things being equal, for any given price the buyer should opt for the acquisition method that yields the lowest NPTC (but see paragraph 4.202). Let us take a look at a few examples to flesh out the concept.

EXAMPLE 4A   *XYZ Corporation buys all of the assets and assumes all of the liabilities of ABC Corporation for their market value ($1,000) in an Asset Acquisition. The assumed fair market values of the assets purchased (and therefore the tax basis of the assets to the acquiring company) are as follows:*

	Assumed Fair Market Values
Accounts receivable	$ 100
Inventory	400
Land	200
Machinery and equipment	500
Accounts payable	(200)
	$1,000

Based on paragraph B.401a, we know that the machinery and equipment is five-year ACRS property. The depreciation deductions (calculated using the five-year ACRS depreciation percentages in paragraph B.401b) and tax savings assuming that the acquiring company has sufficient income against which to offset these deductions and a tax rate of 50 percent are as follows:

	Year 1	Year 2	Year 3	Year 4	Year 5
Depreciation deductions	$75	$110	$105	$105	$105
Assumed tax rate	50%	50%	50%	50%	50%
Tax savings	$38	$ 55	$ 53	$ 53	$ 53

In order to determine the NPTC we have to discount the tax savings back to the date of the acquisition and subtract them from the initial cost. But what rate should we use to discount the tax savings? We could argue for using a number of rates including the acquiring company's borrowing rate or its weighted-average cost of capital. A firm's **weighted-average cost of capital (WACC)** *is defined as the weighted average of the costs of debt, preferred and common stock. The WACC reflects the current cost of raising an additional dollar of the various components and not the historical cost of the various components. However, if there is little risk that the tax savings will be realized, it is probably prudent to use the five-year Treasury bill (risk free) rate adjusted upward slightly to reflect some risk. For purposes of this example we will assume the five-year Treasury bill rate is 8 ½–9 percent, so we will use a 10 percent rate to discount the savings.*

	Tax Savings	10 Percent Discount Factor	Present Value
Year 1	$38	.9091	$ 35
Year 2	55	.8264	45
Year 3	53	.7513	40
Year 4	53	.6830	36
Year 5	53	.6209	33
Present value of tax savings			$189

Calculation of NPTC

Purchase price	$1,000
Less: Present value of tax savings	(189)
NPTC	$ 811

EXAMPLE 4B *XYZ Corporation buys all of the stock of ABC Corporation for $1,000 in a Stock Acquisition. As we know from paragraph 3.301b, the acquiring company will only be able to continue to depreciate the adjusted basis of the assets purchased in this type of acquisition. The basis of the assets of the target company are listed below.*

	Adjusted Basis
Accounts receivable	$100
Inventory	200
Land	50
Machinery and equipment	200
Accounts payable	(200)
	$350

We will assume that the machinery and equipment was all purchased five years ago at a cost of $733 and is being depreciated over 10 years using the sum-of-the-years'-digits depreciation method (see paragraph B.403b). The depreciation deductions and tax savings associated therewith are developed below.

Year after Acquisition	Depreciation Year	Calculation	Depreciation Deduction
1	6th year	$(733 × 5/55)	$ 67
2	7th year	(733 × 4/55)	53
3	8th year	(733 × 3/55)	40
4	9th year	(733 × 2/55)	27
5	10th year	(733 × 1/55)	13
Total deductions			$200

We will assume that XYZ Corporation also should use a 10 percent discount rate.

	Year 1	*Year 2*	*Year 3*	*Year 4*	*Year 5*
Depreciation deductions	$67	$53	$40	$27	$13
Assumed tax rate	50%	50%	50%	50%	50%
Tax savings	$34	$27	$20	$14	$ 7

	Tax Savings	*10 percent Discount Factor*	*Present Value*
Year 1	$34	.9091	$31
Year 2	27	.8264	22
Year 3	20	.7513	15
Year 4	14	.6830	10
Year 5	7	.6209	4
Present value of tax savings			$82

Calculation of NPTC

Purchase price	$1,000
Less: Present value of tax savings	(82)
NPTC	$ 918

The examples above give us an idea of how the concept of NPTC works. However, there are a number of practical problems to address in performing the calculations. For instance, how did we get the fair market value of the machinery and equipment in the first example, especially if we are early in the negotiations? The answer is that we took our best guess. In putting together the acquisition model described later in this book, executives are forced to come up with estimates for a number of variables. The cost analysis described in this section dictates that they do the same for variables that directly affect the company's future tax burden. It is an inexact science, yet going through the exercise yields two substantial benefits: (1) it enables management to take a posture in negotiations regarding the method of consummating the acquisition and (2) it sensitizes management to the effect that a change in their opinion as to the value of certain assets will have on the NPTC of the acquisition. The author realizes that allocating purchase price values to individual assets as part of the analysis of the target is a significant departure from prior practice in analyzing acquisitions in many instances. Yet, the author knows of no other way to calculate the true economic cost of the acquisition to the acquiring company.

4.202   Nontax Factors Affecting Buyer

The buyer must also consider certain nontax factors in deciding on how to effect a transaction. In some cases these factors will dictate that a particular method be employed, even if that method will result in a greater NPTC to the buyer. These nontax considerations generally involve legal requirements that must be met in effecting a transaction as a stock deal, asset deal or merger/consolidation. The discussion below focuses on the advantages and disadvantages of each type of transaction. These legal requirements apply regardless of whether a deal is taxable or nontaxable.

4.202a Stock Deal

Advantages

1. This type of deal is the least complex in terms of the documents that must be prepared. Basically all that is involved is a transfer of stock certificates in exchange for immediate (or sometimes deferred) payment.
2. Due to the simplicity of the deal, it can be accomplished very quickly.
3. A stock deal can be executed over the objections of the target's management through a tender offer.
4. The fact that controlling shareholders have sold their stock does not automatically give minority shareholders appraisal rights.
5. Generally, shareholder votes authorizing the purchase or the sale are not required.

Disadvantages

1. The acquiring company purchasing the stock of the target purchases the target subject to all of its liabilities whether disclosed or undisclosed, contingent or otherwise.
2. A tender offer may be opposed by the target's management.
3. Although the minority shareholders do not ordinarily have appraisal rights, the acquiring company must still deal with them.
4. If the acquiring company plans to liquidate the target company subsequent to the acquisition, there will be a substantial amount of work involved in conveying all of the target company's assets as part of the liquidation.

4.202b Asset Deal

Advantages

1. In an asset deal the acquiring company has complete control over the assets it will purchase and the liabilities it will assume.
2. Generally, a shareholder vote by the acquiring company is not required.

Disadvantages

1. An asset purchase is the most complex transaction to effect because every asset must be separately conveyed.
2. Transaction must comply with Bulk Sales laws.
3. Have to be careful not to violate creditors rights. Also may need consents to certain transfers and assignments.
4. Requires substantial favorable vote of shareholders of the target company.
5. State and local transfer taxes.
6. Possibly greater disruption of customers and suppliers.

4.202c Merger or Consolidation

Advantages

1. Relatively straightforward procedures.
2. Assets transferred by operation of law.
3. No minority interest in the target company remains.

Disadvantages

1. The acquiring company assumes all the liabilities of the target whether disclosed or undisclosed, contingent or otherwise.
2. Any representations and warranties made on behalf of the target company do not survive the transaction.
3. Dissenting minority shareholders of both the acquiring and target companies have appraisal rights.
4. Shareholders of both the acquiring and target companies must vote to approve the transaction.
5. The target company loses its identity.

4.3 SELLER'S PERSPECTIVE

Although this paragraph deals with the seller's perspective in a transaction, it is must reading for the buyer because he must understand the consequences the seller is faced with in a transaction. This knowledge always works to his advantage in negotiations.

4.301 Net Present Proceeds (NPP)

In general, the seller wants the transaction effected using a method that will maximize its Net Present Proceeds or NPP. The **NPP** are defined as the value of all cash and cash equivalents, plus the present value of all other forms of consideration, less the present value of the tax burden that the seller will bear as a result of the transaction. The examples below illustrate the concept.

EXAMPLE 4C *XYZ Corporation purchases all of the assets and liabilities of ABC Corporation for $1,000 in an Asset Acquisition. The target company plans to liquidate in a 337 Liquidation after the transaction. The target is owned by a single stockholder who has a basis of $700 in his stock. He has held the stock for several years. The parties agree on the fair market values of the assets as listed below. ABC Corporation's basis for each asset and related gain also appear.*

	Fair Market Value	Adjusted Basis	Taxable Gain
Accounts receivable	$ 100	$100	
Inventory	400	400	
Land	200	50	$150
Machinery and equipment	500	200	300
Accounts payable	(200)	(200)	
	$1,000	$550	$450

We will assume that the machinery and equipment was all purchased 5 years ago at a cost of $733 and was being depreciated over 10 years using sum-of-the- years'-digits depreciation method. We will also assume that a 10 percent investment tax credit was taken on the property when it was first placed in service. As a result of the transaction, ABC Corporation will have the following depreciation and investment tax credit recapture due to the rules described in paragraphs B.405b and B.508:

Depreciation Recapture

	Gross Value	Accumulated Depreciation Deductions	Adjusted Basis	Sales Price	Taxable Gain	Section 1245 Recapture Income*
Machinery and equipment	$733	$533	$200	$500	$300	$300

*Lesser of taxable gain or accumulated depreciation deductions.

Investment Tax Credit Recapture

Asset	Full Years of Service	Useful Life	ITC Taken	Recapture Percentage	ITC Recapture
Machinery and equipment	5	10	$73	33.3%	$24

Calculation of ABC's Tax Burden

Depreciation recapture	$300	
Assumed tax rate	50%	
Tax on depreciation recaptured	150	$150
Investment tax credit recapture		24
Total tax burden		$174

Example 4C

Calculation of NPP to ABC

Selling price	$1,000
Less: Tax burden	(174)
NPP to ABC	$ 826

Calculation of Stockholder's Tax Burden*

Proceeds available for distribution	$826
Tax basis of stock	700
Taxable gain before exclusion	126
Long term capital gain exclusion	
($126 × 60%)	76
Taxable gain	$ 50
Assumed tax rate	50%
Tax burden on stockholder	$ 25

*Exclusive of any burden associated with the minimum tax rules or the corporate tax preference cutback. See paragraph B. 9.

Calculation of NPP to Stockholder

Liquidation proceeds	$826
Less: Tax burden	(25)
NPP to stockholder	$801

EXAMPLE 4D *XYZ Corporation buys all of the stock of ABC Corporation for $1,000 in a Stock Acquisition. ABC's stock is owned by one person who has a basis in the stock of $700. The person has owned the stock for several years. The person's NPP from the sale are as follows:*

Calculation of Stockholder's Tax Burden*

Sale price	$1,000
Tax basis of stock	700
Taxable gain	300
Long-term capital gain exclusion	
($300 × 60%)	(180)
Taxable gain	120
Assumed tax rate	50%
Tax burden to stockholder	$ 60

*Exclusive of any burden associated with the minimum tax rules or the corporate tax preference cutback. See paragraph B. 9.

Calculation of NPP to Stockholder

Sale price	$1,000
Less: Tax burden	(60)
NPP to stockholder	$ 940

The examples illustrate the concept of NPP. The calculations in the examples are difficult for the buyer to perform because it is unlikely that the buyer will ever know the seller's tax basis for his stock. Moreover, if the target company is willing to sell assets in an Asset Acquisition, it is unlikely that the buyer will learn of the seller's tax basis in its assets. However, to the extent that any other method of acquisition is contemplated, the buyer can rightfully request the prior tax returns for the target company and obtain the asset basis information. It is also important that the buyer make a best guess at the seller's stock basis and perform the analysis described so that he has an understanding of the transaction as the seller sees it.

Let us look at one final example concerning a nontaxable transaction.

EXAMPLE 4E *XYZ Corporation, a publicly owned company, purchases all of the stock of ABC Corporation in a Type B Reorganization. The sole stockholder, who is 68 years old, receives voting common stock of XYZ Corporation valued at $25 million in exchange for his stock in ABC Corporation, a company he started 40 years ago with $5,000. The stockholder's basis in his stock is estimated to be less than $2 million. If the stockholder holds the stock of XYZ until death, his heirs will receive a basis in the XYZ stock equal to its fair market value at the date of death. Assuming they sold the XYZ stock immediately thereafter, they would not have any tax liability because there would be no gain or loss on the sale. A nontaxable transaction such as this is an excellent estate planning technique because it converts a nonliquid asset into a publicly traded stock as well as eliminating a large potential tax liability. However, this type of transaction is not without real economic risk. The seller has exchanged his shares for stock in a company whose value may fluctuate widely.*

4.302   Nontax Factors Affecting Seller

The seller is affected by certain nontax factors in deciding on an acquisition method. These factors generally involve legal requirements for effecting a transaction. The discussion below deals with the advantages and disadvantages of a stock deal, asset deal, or merger/consolidation.

4.302a   Stock Deal

Advantages

1. A stock deal is relatively simple. The seller exchanges his stock for consideration.
2. Since a stock deal is simple, it can be executed quickly.
3. Management's opinion does not stop the stockholder from selling stock.
4. Minority shareholders cannot generally prevent a controlling shareholder from selling stock.

5. A shareholder vote is not required.

6. This transaction gives the acquiring company responsibility for all liabilities.

Disadvantages

1. The transaction may require SEC registration.

2. A seller of a control position may owe a fiduciary duty to minority shareholders.

4.302b   Asset Deal

Advantages

1. Straightforward sale.

2. Usually for cash or cash and notes.

3. Does not receive stock of acquiring company.

Disadvantages

1. Complex transaction where each asset must be separately conveyed.

2. Transaction must comply with Bulk Sales law.

3. Have to be careful not to violate creditors' rights. Also may need consents for certain transfers and assignments.

4. Shareholders must approve transaction.

5. State and local transfer taxes.

6. Does not receive stock of acquiring company.

4.302c   Merger or Consolidation

Advantages

1. Relatively straightforward procedures.

2. Assets transferred by operation of law.

3. Wide range of consideration that can be received.

4. Participation in future growth through proprietary interest in merged entity.

Disadvantages

1. Dissenting minority shareholders of both acquiring company and target company have appraisal rights.

2. Shareholders of both target and acquiring companies must approve merger/consolidation.

3. Target company loses its identity.

4. Participation in future growth through proprietary interest in merged entity.

Chapter 5

Comparing Acquisition Methods

5.1 INTRODUCTION

The previous chapter laid the foundation for calculating the real economic cost and proceeds of an acquisition. This chapter describes how to complete an analysis that compares the real cost and proceeds under different acquisition methods and purchase prices. In most cases the parties interested in completing a transaction do not wish to consider all six alternate forms of effecting a transaction. The three nontaxable transactions are of interest only in certain circumstances. Furthermore, due to an overriding nontax consideration, a transaction may have to be effected in a particular manner. A fortunate result of this elimination of unattractive alternatives is that the amount of financial analysis necessary is usually limited to a comparative analysis of two or three methods. Nevertheless, for illustrative purposes this chapter will compare all six methods of effecting a transaction using a common example.

5.2 COMPARATIVE ANALYSIS

The theory underlying comparative analysis is that the decision maker understands an Asset Acquisition because it generally reflects the standard purchase situation (see paragraph 1.1). Given that the decision maker understands the true economic cost in an Asset Acquisition, the other methods can be compared to it.

Comparative analysis is typically not required where an acquisition is contemplated to be an Asset Acquisition from the start of negotiations. In that case, an analysis of the Net Present Tax Cost (NPTC) and Net Present Proceeds (NPP) at various purchase prices should suffice.

5.201   Common Example

The remainder of the chapter consists of a comparative analysis of a relatively simple example. Although this example is straightforward, it provides the framework for handling much more complex problems.

EXAMPLE 5A   *XYZ Corporation enters into negotiations with ABC Corporation to purchase its business. XYZ Corporation is a Fortune 500 company with a good track record in acquisitions. ABC Corporation is a public corporation. However, 40 percent of the stock is held by one family. The family consists of three young children and parents both in their mid-50s who started the business 26 years ago. Both parents are in excellent health. However, neither believes that their children will be interested in the business and are therefore looking to sell out. The business has been very profitable over recent years and has the following current balance sheet:*

ABC CORPORATION
Interim Balance Sheet as of November 30, 1984
(In Millions)

Assets		Liabilities	
Cash and accounts		Accounts payable and	
receivable	$100	accrued expenses	$200
Inventory	200	*Stockholders' Equity*	
Land	50		
Buildings and improvements	100	Common stock	50
Machinery and equipment	250	Retained earnings	450
		Total liabilities and	
Total assets	$700	stockholders' equity	$700

We will assume that the prospective deal would close on January 1, 1985, the first day of both companies' fiscal year.

5.3   ASSET ACQUISITION

Initially we will assume that the transaction, for some reason, must be consummated as an Asset Acquisition. The first step in the analysis is to estimate a purchase price range. Based on a number of factors including other comparable sales, ABC's earnings history, and general stock market conditions, XYZ estimates that an asset deal for all assets and liabilities would cost between $800 million to $1,200 million. Having chosen the purchase price range, the specific purchase prices to be analyzed must be determined. Furthermore, an allocation of value to the various asset categories must be completed based on available information.

After consulting with various members of XYZ's organization, the financial staff was able to come up with preliminary estimates of the fair market value for all assets and liabilities for the selected purchase prices it would analyze (see Illustration 1).

Illustration 1
Allocation of Purchase Price to Asset Categories *(In Millions)*

	\$800	\$1,000	\$1,200
	Purchase Price		
Cash and accounts receivable	\$100	\$ 100	\$ 100
Inventory	200	200	200
Land	200	200	200
Buildings and improvements	200	225	250
Machinery and equipment	300	450	500
Goodwill	0	25	150
Accounts payable and accrued expenses	(200)	(200)	(200)
	\$800	\$1,000	\$1,200

Due to the preliminary nature of these estimates, it is reasonable to assume that the fair market values of certain assets (e.g., buildings and improvements, machinery and equipment, and goodwill) would be greater given a higher purchase price. Why? If a buyer is willing to pay a higher price, this generally indicates that he has higher expectations of the profit potential to be generated by the business' assets. Given this higher profit expectancy, the underlying business assets have more value to him. One might argue that any increase in value over the bottom figures is all attributable to the company's goodwill, but this probably does not reflect reality. Remember, these are preliminary estimates. If hard information (appraisals) were available as to the fair market values of the assets, this information should be used. If the sum of the appraised values differs from the assumed purchase price, then (1) a second tier allocation must be performed to determine the tax basis of the various asset categories (see paragraph 3.203) and (2) an allocation of value must be performed to determine the book value of the various asset categories (see paragraph C.201).

5.301 NPTC

The next step is to compute the NPTC to the buyer under the alternate purchase prices. We will assume that the buyer had adequate taxable income to offset any deductions associated with ABC's operation. We will also assume that XYZ should discount the tax savings associated with the acquisition at 10 percent (see paragraph 4.201). Finally, the analysis will go forward only 10 years because XYZ believes this is a reasonable time frame over which to perform the business forecast.

In order to reach the NPTC we must calculate the depreciation deductions and related tax savings for the buildings and improvements and the machinery and equipment. These calculations are given in Illustrations 2 and 3.

Illustration 2
Calculation of the Net Present Value of the Tax Savings from the Depreciation Deductions for Buildings and Improvements *(Dollar Figures in Millions)*

	Year	$800	$1,000	$1,200
Total purchase price				
Fair market value of buildings and improvements		200	225	250
ACRS depreciation percentages	1	9%	9%	9%
for 18-year class of property	2	9	9	9
	3	8	8	8
	4	7	7	7
	5	6	6	6
	6	6	6	6
	7	5	5	5
	8	5	5	5
	9	5	5	5
	10	5	5	5
Depreciation deductions	1	$ 18	$ 20	$ 23
	2	18	20	23
	3	16	18	20
	4	14	16	18
	5	12	14	15
	6	12	14	15
	7	10	11	13
	8	10	11	13
	9	10	11	13
	10	10	11	13
Tax savings at 50%	1	9	10	11
	2	9	10	11
	3	8	9	10
	4	7	8	9
	5	6	7	8
	6	6	7	8
	7	5	6	6
	8	5	6	6
	9	5	6	6
	10	5	6	6
10% present value factors	1	.9091	.9091	.9091
	2	.8264	.8264	.8264
	3	.7513	.7513	.7513
	4	.6830	.6830	.6830
	5	.6209	.6209	.6209
	6	.5645	.5645	.5645
	7	.5132	.5132	.5132
	8	.4665	.4665	.4665
	9	.4241	.4241	.4241
	10	.3855	.3855	.3855

Illustration 2 (concluded)

	Year	$800	$1,000	$1,200
Total purchase price				
Fair market value of buildings and improvements		200	225	250
Present value of tax savings	1	8	9	10
	2	7	8	9
	3	6	7	8
	4	5	5	6
	5	4	4	5
	6	3	4	4
	7	3	3	3
	8	2	3	3
	9	2	2	3
	10	2	2	2
		42	48	53

Illustration 3
Calculation of the Net Present Value of the Tax Savings from the Depreciation Deductions for Machinery and Equipment *(Dollar Figures in Millions)*

	Year	$800	$1,000	$1,200
Total Purchase Price				
Fair market value of machinery and equipment		300	450	500
ACRS depreciation percentages for 5-year class of property	1	15%	15%	15%
	2	22	22	22
	3	21	21	21
	4	21	21	21
	5	21	21	21
Depreciation deductions	1	45	68	75
	2	66	99	110
	3	63	95	105
	4	63	95	105
	5	63	95	105
Tax savings at 50%	1	23	34	38
	2	33	50	55
	3	32	47	53
	4	32	47	53
	5	32	47	53
10% present value factors	1	.9091	.9091	.9091
	2	.8264	.8264	.8264
	3	.7513	.7513	.7513
	4	.6830	.6830	.6830
	5	.6209	.6209	.6209
Present value of tax savings	1	$ 20	$ 31	$ 34
	2	27	41	45
	3	24	35	39
	4	22	32	36
	5	20	29	33
		$ 112	$ 169	$ 187

Now that we have computed the present value of the future tax savings associated with depreciation deductions, we can calculate the NPTC for the buyer under the various purchase prices being analyzed (see Illustration 4). As indicated, the buyer's NPTC will range between $646 and $960 million.

Illustration 4
Asset Acquisition—Calculation of NPTC *(In Millions)*

	$800	$1,000	$1,200
Purchase price	$800	$1,000	$1,200
Less: Present value of tax savings for			
machinery and equipment	(112)	(169)	(187)
Building and improvements	(42)	(48)	(53)
NPTC	$646	$ 783	$ 960

5.302   NPP

Once the analysis of the NPTC to the buyer has been completed, the buyer should estimate the NPP to the seller. This analysis is difficult to perform because the buyer does not know (1) the tax basis of the seller's assets, (2) whether or not the stockholders of the target intend to liquidate the target in a 337 Liquidation, or (3) the basis of the target's stock to the shareholders. However, based on a review of the figures and discussions with ABC officials, the buyer came up with the necessary estimates (see Illustrations 5 and 6).

Illustration 5
ABC Corporation's Capital Expenditures *(In Millions)*

	1978	1979	1980	1981	1982	1983	1984E
Buildings and improvements	10	30			10		
Machinery and equipment	16	14	18	13	17	23	20
Total expenditures	$ 26	$ 44	$ 18	$ 13	$ 27	$ 23	$ 20
Estimated investment tax credits taken	$1.6	$1.4	$1.8	$1.3	$1.7	$2.3	$2.0

The NPP to be received by the seller includes the value of all cash and cash equivalents plus the present value of all other forms of consideration less the present value of the tax burden that the seller will bear, either presently or in the future, as a result of the transaction. In this case, the purchase prices to analyze have already been selected. Therefore, what remains to be done is to calculate the tax burden to the seller at the different prices. Due to the fact that the buyer does not know

Illustration 6
Selected Book and Tax Values at November 30, 1984 *(In Millions)*

	Book Value	Estimated Tax Basis
Buildings and improvements—gross	$350	$350
Accumulated depreciation	250	300
Buildings and improvements—net	$100	$ 50
Machinery and equipment—gross	$450	$450
Accumulated depreciation	200	350
Machinery and equipment—net	$250	$100
Shareholders estimated tax basis in ABC Corporation stock		$300

whether or not the seller intends to liquidate ABC Corporation, two analyses must be done: (1) an analysis assuming no liquidation and (2) an analysis assuming liquidation.

There are two important facts to remember about a 337 Liquidation. First, generally no gains or losses are recognized by the selling corporation if it has adopted a plan of liquidation. Second, the selling corporation will recognize LIFO investment credit and depreciation recapture (see paragraph 3.201c).

The calculations common to both analyses are given in Illustrations 7 and 8. These include calculations of depreciation recapture and investment tax credit recapture. We will assume there is no LIFO recapture. XYZ estimates that ABC depreciated its buildings on a straight line basis for tax purposes, and therefore there is no depreciation recapture related to this asset category. See paragraph B.405 for a complete discussion of depreciation recapture, paragraph B.304 for a discussion of the interplay of Section 1231 with the depreciation recapture provisions, and paragraph B.508 for a review of the recapture of investment

Illustration 7
Depreciation Recapture for Machinery and Equipment *(In Millions)*

Total purchase price	$800	$1,000	$1,200
Fair market value of machinery and equipment	$300	$ 450	$ 500
Adjusted basis	100	100	100
Realized gain	$200	$ 350	$ 400
Accumulated depreciation	$350	$ 350	$ 350
Section 1245 recapture income*	$200	$ 350	$ 350
Section 1231 gain			50
Recognized gain	$200	$ 350	$ 400

*Lesser of realized gain or accumulated depreciation.

Illustration 8
Investment Tax Credit Recapture for Machinery and Equipment
(In Millions)

Year Placed in Service	Useful Life	Class of Property	Estimated ITC Taken	Recapture Percentage	ITC Recapture
1978	7+		1.6	33.3%	.53
1979	7+		1.4	33.3	.47
1980	7+		1.8	66.6	1.20
1981		5-year	1.3	40.0	.52
1982		5-year	1.7	60.0	1.02
1983		5-year	2.3	80.0	1.84
1984		5-year	2.0	100.0	2.00
				Total	7.58
				Say	8.00

tax credits (ITC). The net result of the calculations is that the estimated ITC recapture is $8 million, the Section 1245 depreciation recaptured amounts to between $200 and $350 million, and there is Section 1231 gain of $50 million if the purchase price is $1.2 billion.

The Gain on Net Assets Sold Schedule calculates the taxable gain at various prices and the character of any gain (see Illustration 9). Let us review the calculations for the $1.2 billion purchase price. Cash, accounts receivable, and inventory are purchased at a price equal to their adjusted basis so there is no gain or loss associated with these items. The depreciation recapture and Section 1231 income amounts associated with machinery and equipment have been calculated in a schedule above and are merely repeated here for completeness. Land and buildings and improvements are both Section 1231 assets. Therefore, the gain associated with either is Section 1231 income. Note that there is no depreciation recapture associated with the buildings and improvements because these assets were assumed to have been depreciated on a straight line basis (see paragraph B.405). Goodwill is a capital asset (not a Section 1231 asset) in the hands of the target. Therefore, the gain associated with its sale is capital gain. Finally, there is no taxable gain on the assumption of ABC's liabilities.

ABC's tax burden is calculated in Illustration 10. This tax burden potentially has three components: (1) the ordinary income tax due on the Section 1245 recapture income (see paragraph B.405), (2) the tax calculated at the capital gains rate on the sum of the Section 1231 gain and any long-term capital gain (see paragraph B.3), and (3) the tax due on the recapture of investment tax credits (see paragraph B.7). If ABC Corporation liquidates under Section 337, then its tax burden is only the sum of (1) and (3) above; whereas if it does not liquidate, its tax burden is the sum of all three components.

Illustration 9   Asset Acquisition—Gain on Net Assets Sold (In Millions)

	(A) Gross Book Value	(B) Accumulated Depreciation	(C) Adjusted Basis (A)−(B)	(D) Fair Market Value	(E) Taxable Gain (D)−(C)	(F) Section 1245 Recapture Income Lesser of (B) or (E)	(G) Section 1231 Income (D)−(F)	(H) Capital Gain
						Character of Gain		
$800 Purchase Price								
Cash and accounts receivable	$100		$100	$ 100				
Inventory	200		200	200				
Machinery and equipment	450	$350	100	300	$200	$200		
Land	50		50	200	150		$150	
Buildings and improvements	350	300	50	200	150		150	
Goodwill								—
Accounts payable and accrued expenses	(200)		(200)	(200)				—
Totals	$950	$650	$300	$ 800	$500	$200	$300	
$1,000 Purchase Price								
Cash and accounts receivable	$100		$100	$ 100				
Inventory	200		200	200				
Machinery and equipment	450	$350	100	450	$350	$350		
Land	50		50	200	150		$150	
Buildings and improvements	350	300	50	225	175		175	
Goodwill				25	25			$ 25
Accounts payable and accrued expenses	(200)		(200)	(200)				
Totals	$950	$650	$300	$1,000	$700	$350	$325	$ 25
$1,200 Purchase Price								
Cash and accounts receivable	$100		$100	$ 100				
Inventory	200		200	200				
Machinery and equipment	450	$350	100	500	$400	$350	$ 50	
Land	50		50	200	150		150	
Buildings and improvements	350	300	50	250	200		200	
Goodwill				150	150			$150
Accounts payable and accrued expenses	(200)		(200)	(200)				
Totals	$950	$650	$300	$1,200	$900	$350	$400	$150

Illustration 10
ABC Corporation's Tax Burden *(In Millions)** *

Total purchase price	$ 800	$1,000	$1,200
Tax basis of net assets	300	300	300
Taxable gain	$ 500	$ 700	$ 900
Section 1245 recapture income	$ 200	$ 350	$ 350
Assumed tax rate	50%	50%	50%
Tax burden—(1)	$ 100	$ 175	$ 175
Section 1231 gain	$ 300	$ 325	$ 400
Long-term capital gain	___	25	150
Total gain	300	350	550
Capital gains tax rate	28%	28%	28%
Tax burden—(2)	$ 84	$ 98	$ 154
Recapture of ITC—(3)	$ 8	$ 8	$ 8
Total tax burden—(1)+(2)+(3)	$ 192	$ 281	$ 337
Total tax burden—(1)+(3)	$ 108	$ 183	$ 183

*Exclusive of any burden associated with the minimum tax rules or the corporate tax preference cut back. See paragraph B. 9.

ABC Corporation's NPP are calculated in Illustration 11 under both the liquidation and nonliquidation assumptions. If ABC does not liquidate, it will realize between $608 and $863 million on the sale; whereas if it does liquidate, the shareholders will receive between $692 and $1,017 million in proceeds.

Illustration 11
Asset Acquisition—Calculation of NPP to ABC Corporation
(In Millions)

Assuming no liquidation:			
Selling price	$800	$1,000	$1,200
Less: Tax burden	192	281	337
NPP	$608	$ 719	$ 863
Assuming liquidation:			
Selling price	$800	$1,000	$1,200
Less: Tax burden	108	183	183
NPP	$692	$ 817	$1,017

If ABC Corporation completely liquidates, the shareholders will be treated for tax purposes as if they sold their stock for an amount equal to the proceeds received. Assuming that the stock is a capital asset in their hands and has been held longer than the required holding period, the shareholders will be taxed at the capital gains rate (see paragraph B.3). The schedule in Illustration 12 calculates this tax burden to the shareholders.

The final schedule in Illustration 13 calculates the NPP to ABC's stockholders assuming the company is liquidated. After payment of their tax burden on the liquidation, the stockholders' NPP will be between $613 and $873 million.

Illustration 12
Calculation of Stockholder's Tax Burden Assuming Liquidation
(In Millions) [*]

	$800	$1,000	$1,200
Selling price			
Proceeds available for distribution	$692	$ 817	$1,017
Tax basis of stock	300	300	300
Taxable gain before exclusion	392	517	717
Long-term capital gain exclusion at 60%	235	310	430
Taxable gain	157	207	287
Tax rate	50%	50%	50%
Tax burden on stockholders	$ 79	$ 104	$ 144

[*]Exclusive of any burden associated with the minimum tax rules or the corporate tax preference cut back. See paragraph 9. B.

Illustration 13
Asset Acquisition—Calculation of NPP to Stockholders *(In Millions)*

	$800	$1,000	$1,200
Selling Price			
Liquidation proceeds	$692	$ 817	$1.017
Less: Tax burden	(79)	(104)	(144)
NPP	$613	$ 713	$ 873

5.303 Presentation of Results

Having completed the NPTC to XYZ Corporation and the NPP to ABC Corporation and its stockholders, all that remains is to present the results in a format that is easy to understand. The graph in Illustration 14 hopefully conveys in a meaningful manner the results. XYZ's NPTC will be between $646 and $960 million if an Asset Acquisition is consummated within the range of purchase prices analyzed. ABC's NPP (assuming no liquidation) from such a transaction would be between $608 and $863 million, and ABC's stockholders NPP (assuming liquidation) would be somewhere between $613 and $873 million.

Illustration 14

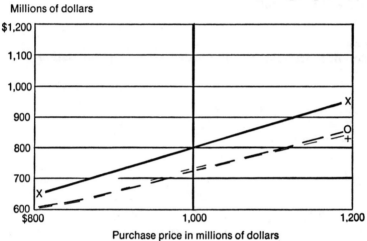

ASSET ACQUISITION

Net Present Tax Cost (NPTC) to XYZ Corporation versus Net Present Proceeds (NPP) to ABC Corporation Assuming No Liquidation and ABC Corporation's Stockholders Assuming Liquidation

Millions of dollars

Purchase price in millions of dollars

X = NPTC   O = Stockholder's NPP   + = ABC Corporation's NPP

5.4   338 TRANSACTION

In analyzing the deal as a 338 Transaction we will assume that XYZ will purchase all of the outstanding stock of ABC, and that XYZ has decided to analyze the same price range $800–$1,200, even though it is a different type of deal.

5.401   NPTC

The first step in analyzing this type of deal is to calculate the NPTC. We know from paragraph 3.202b that the acquiring company will take a basis in the assets of the target company equal to the price paid for the stock adjusted for the amount of depreciation and investment tax credits recaptured. An upward adjustment in the basis of the target's assets is allowed for any recapture tax paid because the IRS realizes that it is a real cost to the acquiring company. It should be noted that in this type of acquisition the buyer should be able to get data on the tax basis of assets and tax credits which can be used to calculate recapture liability.

Illustration 15
Calculation of Adjusted Purchase Price *(In Millions)*

Purchase price	$800	$1,000	$1,200
Section 1245 recapture tax*	100	175	175
Investment tax credits recaptured*	8	8	8
Adjusted purchase price	$908	$1,183	$1,383

*Calculated in paragraph 5.302.

The calculation of the adjusted purchase price for the stock is shown in Illustration 15. Based on these adjusted purchase prices the buyer came up with the following preliminary allocations of the adjusted purchase price to the various asset categories (see Illustration 16). As discussed previously, it is reasonable to assume that the fair market values of certain assets (e.g., buildings and improvements, machinery and equipment, and goodwill) would be greater given a higher purchase price. Why? If a buyer is willing to pay a higher price, this generally indicates that he has higher expectations of the profit potential to be generated by the business' assets. Given this higher profit expectancy, the underlying business assets have more value to him. One might argue that any increase in value over the bottom figures is all attributable to the company's goodwill, but this probably does not reflect reality. Remember, these are preliminary estimates. If hard information (appraisals) were available as to the fair market values of the assets, this information should be used. If the sum of the appraised values differs from the assumed adjusted purchase price, then (1) a second tier allocation must be performed to determine the tax basis of the various asset categories (see paragraph 3.203) and (2) an allocation of value must be performed to determine the book value of the various asset categories (see paragraph C.201).

XYZ's NPTC includes its adjusted purchase price for the stock reduced by the present value of the tax savings associated with depreciat-

Illustration 16
Allocation of Adjusted Purchase Price to Asset Categories *(In Millions)*

	Purchase Price		
	$800	$1,000	$1,200
Cash and accounts receivable	$100	$ 100	$ 100
Inventory	200	200	200
Land	200	200	200
Buildings and improvements	200	250	250
Machinery and equipment	400	500	500
Goodwill	33	133	333
Accounts payable and accrued expenses	(200)	(200)	(200)
	$908	$1,183	$1,383

ing the buildings and improvements and the machinery and equipment. In computing the depreciation on the buildings and improvements and the machinery and equipment, the tax basis used will be based on the schedule given in Illustration 16, which allocates the adjusted purchase price to the various asset categories (see Illustrations 17 and 18).

Illustration 17
Calculation of the Net Present Value of the Tax Savings from the Depreciation Deductions for Buildings and Improvements *(Dollar Figures in Millions)*

	Year	$800	$1,000	$1,200
Total purchase price		$800	$1,000	$1,200
Fair market value of buildings and improvements		200	250	250
ACRS depreciation percentages for 18-year class of property	1	9%	9%	9%
	2	9	9	9
	3	8	8	8
	4	7	7	7
	5	6	6	6
	6	6	6	6
	7	5	5	5
	8	5	5	5
	9	5	5	5
	10	5	5	5
Depreciation deductions	1	$ 18	$ 23	$ 23
	2	18	23	23
	3	16	20	20
	4	14	18	18
	5	12	15	15
	6	12	15	15
	7	10	13	13
	8	10	13	13
	9	10	13	13
	10	10	13	13
Tax savings at 50%	1	9	11	11
	2	9	11	11
	3	8	10	10
	4	7	9	9
	5	6	8	8
	6	6	8	8
	7	5	6	6
	8	5	6	6
	9	5	6	6
	10	5	6	6
10% present value factors	1	.9091	.9091	.9091
	2	.8264	.8264	.8264
	3	.7513	.7513	.7513
	4	.6830	.6830	.6830
	5	.6209	.6209	.6209
	6	.5645	.5645	.5645
	7	.5132	.5132	.5132
	8	.4665	.4665	.4665
	9	.4241	.4241	.4241
	10	.3855	.3855	.3855

Illustration 17 (*concluded*)

		$800	$1,000	$1,200
Total purchase price				
Fair market value of buildings and improvements	Year	200	250	250
Present value of tax savings	1	8	10	10
	2	7	9	9
	3	6	8	8
	4	5	6	6
	5	4	5	5
	6	3	4	4
	7	3	3	3
	8	2	3	3
	9	2	3	3
	10	2	2	2
		42	53	53

Illustration 18
Calculation of the Net Present Value of the Tax Savings from the Depreciation Deductions for Machinery and Equipment

(Dollar Figures in Millions)

		$800	$1,000	$1,200
Total purchase price				
Fair market value of machinery and equipment	Year	400	500	500
ACRS depreciation percentages for 5-year class of property	1	15%	15%	15%
	2	22	22	22
	3	21	21	21
	4	21	21	21
	5	21	21	21
Depreciation deductions	1	$ 60	$ 75	$ 75
	2	88	110	110
	3	84	105	105
	4	84	105	105
	5	84	105	105
Tax savings at 50%	1	30	38	38
	2	44	55	55
	3	42	53	53
	4	42	53	53
	5	42	53	53
10% present value factors	1	.9091	.9091	.9091
	2	.8264	.8264	.8264
	3	.7513	.7513	.7513
	4	.6830	.6830	.6830
	5	.6209	.6209	.6209
Present value of tax savings	1	$ 27	$ 34	$ 34
	2	36	45	45
	3	32	39	39
	4	29	36	36
	5	26	33	33
		$ 150	$ 187	$ 187

The acquiring company's NPTC will range between $716 and $1,143 assuming a 338 Transaction is effected at a price between $800 and $1,200 million (see Illustration 19).

Illustration 19
338 Transaction—Calculation of NPTC *(In Millions)*

Purchase price	$800	$1,000	$1,200
Less:			
Present value of tax savings for			
Machinery and equipment	(150)	(187)	(187)
Buildings and improvements	(42)	(53)	(53)
Plus:			
ITC recapture*	8	8	8
Tax on Section 1245*			
depreciation recapture	100	175	175
NPTC	$716	$ 943	$1,143

  *Calculated in paragraph 5.302.

5.402   NPP

Having computed the NPTC for the buyer, the next step is to calculate the seller's NPP. The shareholders are selling their stock in a 338 Transaction. XYZ has estimated that the stockholders' tax basis in their stock is $300. Given that the current capital gains tax rules result in a 20 percent effective rate, the stockholders' tax burden will be between $100 and $180 million (see Illustration 20).

Deducting the tax burden from the selling price, the stockholders will net between $700 and $1,020 million in a 338 Transaction (see Illustration 21).

Illustration 20
Tax Burden to Stockholders *(In Millions)**

Purchase Price	$800	$1,000	$1,200
Tax basis of stock	300	300	300
Taxable gain before exclusion	500	700	900
Long-term capital gain exclusion			
(60% × Applicable number)	300	420	540
Taxable gain	200	280	360
Assumed tax rate	50%	50%	50%
Tax burden to stockholders	$100	$ 140	$ 180

  *Exclusive of any burden associated with the minimum tax rules or the corporate tax preference cut back. See paragraph B. 9.

Illustration 21
338 Transaction—Calculation of NPP to Stockholders *(In Millions)*

Selling price	$800	$1,000	$1,200
Less: Tax burden	(100)	(140)	(180)
NPP	$700	$ 860	$1,020

5.403 Presentation of Results

The NPTC and NPP are displayed in the same format used for an Asset Acquisition. XYZ's NPTC will be between $716 and $1,143 million, whereas ABC's shareholder's NPP will range between $700 and $1,020 million (see Illustration 22).

Illustration 22

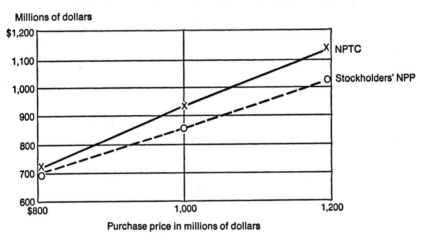

338 TRANSACTION

Net Present Tax Cost (NPTC) to XYZ Corporation versus Net Present Proceeds (NPP) to ABC's Stockholders

Millions of dollars

Purchase price in millions of dollars

5.5 STOCK ACQUISITION

If the transaction is effected as a Stock Acquisition, we will assume that XYZ Corporation will purchase all of the outstanding stock of ABC and that XYZ has decided to analyze the same price range.

5.501 NPTC

The NPTC in this type of deal is equal to the price paid for the stock less the present value of the tax savings from future depreciation deductions calculated using the target company's existing adjusted basis and depreciation methods. Since there will not be a disposition of assets of the target, there will be no depreciation or investment tax credit recapture.

The adjusted basis of the depreciable assets are assumed to be:

Machinery and equipment	$100
Buildings and improvements	50

If this type of deal is contemplated, these figures will be known with certainty because the target company should provide the target company's latest tax returns to the acquirer. We will assume for simplicity that the above assets would be depreciated as shown in Illustration 23.

Illustration 23
Calculation of Present Value of Tax Savings For Depreciable Assets

	Depreciation Deductions				10 Percent	Present
	Machinery and Equipment	Buildings and Improvements	Total	Tax Savings at 50 percent	Present Value Factor	Value of Tax Savings
Year 1	$ 20	$ 8	$ 28	$14	.9091	$13
Year 2	20	7	27	13	.8264	11
Year 3	20	7	27	13	.7513	10
Year 4	20	7	27	13	.6830	9
Year 5	20	7	27	13	.6209	8
Year 6		7	7	3	.5645	2
Year 7		7	7	3	.5132	2
	$100	$50	$150			$55

The NPTC for the buyer can now be calculated (see Illustration 24). XYZ's NPTC will range between $745 and $1,145 assuming a Stock Acquisition is consummated.

Illustration 24
Stock Acquisition—Calculation of NPTC *(In Millions)*

Purchase price	$800	$1,000	$1,200
Less: Present value of tax savings for depreciable assets	(55)	(55)	(55)
NPTC	$745	$945	$1,145

5.502 NPP

The NPP are calculated the same manner as in a 338 Transaction. The calculations are duplicated in Illustrations 25 and 26. ABC Corporation's shareholders NPP will fall between $700 and $1,020 million in a Stock Acquisition.

5.503 Presentation of Results

The results of the analysis appear in a graph in Illustration 27.

Illustration 25
Tax Burden to Stockholders* *(In Millions)*

Selling price	$800	$1,000	$1,200
Tax basis of stock	300	300	300
Taxable gain before exclusion	500	700	900
Long-term capital gain exclusion			
(60% × Applicable number)	300	420	540
Taxable gain	200	280	360
Assumed tax rate	50%	50%	50%
Tax burden	$100	$ 140	$ 180

*Exclusive of any burden associated with the minimum tax rules or the corporate tax prefer-
ence cutback. See paragraph B. 9.

Illustration 26
Stock Acquisition—Calculation of NPP to Stockholders *(In Millions)*

Selling price	$800	$1,000	$1,200
Less: Tax burden	(100)	(140)	(180)
NPP	$700	$ 860	$1,020

Illustration 27

STOCK ACQUISITION

**Net Present Tax Cost (NPTC) to XYZ Corporation versus
Net Present Proceeds (NPP) to ABC's Stockholders**

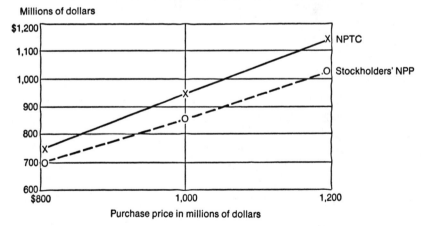

Millions of dollars

Purchase price in millions of dollars

5.6 TYPE A REORGANIZATION

Paragraph 3.302a indicates that there are four different forms of Type A
Reorganizations. For illustrative purposes we will examine a Cash Option Merger executed as a Type A Subsidiary Merger. We will assume

that XYZ wishes to merge the target company into a controlled subsidiary in exchange for stock of XYZ Corporation and cash. At the time of the merger the cash will represent 50 percent of the total consideration paid. The total consideration estimated to close a transaction is in the $800–$1,200 range.

5.601   NPTC

The NPTC in a Type A Reorganization is equal to the market value of securities exchanged plus the fair market value of all other consideration paid less the present value of the tax savings from future depreciation deductions calculated using the target company's existing adjusted basis and depreciation methods. A Type A Reorganization does not give rise to a disposition of assets that would cause depreciation or investment tax credit recapture.

The present value of tax savings from future depreciation deductions is calculated the same as under a Stock Acquisition. The calculations are not repeated here. The NPTC to XYZ Corporation ranges from $745 to $1,145 in this Type A Reorganization (see Illustration 28).

Illustration 28
Type A Reorganization Subsidiary Merger—Calculation of NPTC
(In Millions)

Purchase Price	$800	$1,000	$1,200
Less: Present value of tax savings for depreciable assets	55	55	55
NPTC	$745	$ 945	$1,145

5.602   NPP

Since the stockholders of ABC receive boot in the contemplated transaction, they must reorganize gain to the extent of the lesser of boot received or the gain realized. We will assume that there is no possibility that the cash received constitutes a dividend. Therefore, the gain will be taxed at the capital gains rate. The tax burden amounts to $80 to $120 million (see Illustration 29).

Given the calculated tax burdens, the NPP to ABC's stockholders will range from $720 to $1,080 million (see Illustration 30).

In the calculations in Illustrations 29 and 30, we have assumed that the stockholders of ABC intend to hold onto the stock of XYZ indefinitely. If this were not the case, it would be necessary to present value the estimated sale price of the stock at some time in the future as well as the associated tax burden. It should be noted that the target company's

Illustration 29
Tax Burden to Stockholders* *(In Millions)*

Purchase Price	$800	$1,000	$1,200
Tax basis of stock	300	300	300
Realized gain	500	700	900
Boot received	$400	$ 500	$ 600
Taxable gain before exclusion	$400	$ 500	$ 600
Long-term capital gain exclusion			
(60% × Applicable number)	240	300	360
Taxable gain	160	200	240
Assumed tax rate	50%	50%	50%
Tax burden	$ 80	$ 100	$ 120

*Exclusive of any burden associated with the minimum tax rules or the corporate tax preference cutback. See paragraph B. 9.

Illustration 30
Type A Reorganization Subsidiary Merger—Calculation of NPP to Stockholders *(In Millions)*

Selling Price	$800	$1,000	$1,200
Less Tax burden	(80)	(100)	(120)
NPP	$720	$ 900	$1,080

shareholders are taking on the risk associated with holding the acquiring company's stock. How these shareholders feel about the stability of this investment will heavily influence whether or not they would be interested in this type of transaction.

5.603 Presentation of Results

The results of the analysis are graphed in Illustration 31. XYZ's NPTC ranges from $745 to $1,145 million while ABC's shareholders can expect to receive NPP at $720 to $1,080 million.

5.7 TYPE B REORGANIZATION

Analyzing a Type B Reorganization is very straightforward. In this transaction we will assume XYZ will be able to purchase all the outstanding stock of ABC in a Parent Stock for Stock Transaction.

5.701 NPTC

The NPTC for the acquiring company is equal to the market value of the voting stock exchanged less the present value of the tax savings

Illustration 31

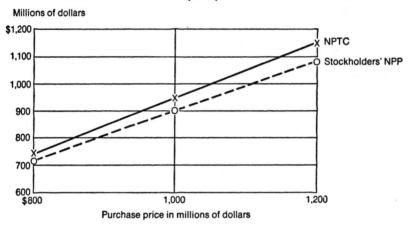

TYPE A REORGANIZATION—SUBSIDIARY MERGER

**Net Present Tax Cost (NPTC) to XYZ Corporation versus
Net Present Proceeds (NPP) to ABC's Stockholders**

from future depreciation deductions calculated using the target company's existing adjusted basis and depreciation methods (see Illustration 32). The present value of the tax savings are the same as those calculated under a Stock Acquisition. XYZ's NPTC in a Type B Reorganization will range from $745 to $1,145 million.

Illustration 32
Type B Reorganization—Calculation of NPTC *(In Millions)*

Purchase Price	$800	$1,000	$1,200
Less: Present value of tax savings for depreciable assets	55	55	55
NPTC	$745	$ 945	$1,145

5.702 NPP

The stockholders of the target company will not have any tax burden associated with this type of transaction unless they intend to liquidate their stock holdings of XYZ at some point. If this is the case, then a calculation should be performed estimating the present value of the proceeds to be received and the associated tax burden. Otherwise, the selling price represents the stockholder's NPP (see Illustration 33). Thus, ABC's stockholders' NPP will be between $800 and $1,200 million. In

Illustration 33
Type B Reorganization—Calculation of NPP to Stockholders
(In Millions)

Selling Price	$800	$1,000	$1,200
NPP	$800	$1,000	$1,200

this transaction the target company's stockholders are assuming the risk associated with holding the acquiring company's stock. Their feelings about such an investment will determine whether or not they are interested in this type of transaction.

5.703 Presentation of Results

The analysis above is graphed in Illustration 34. XYZ's NPTC is between $745 and $1,145 million while ABC's shareholders' NPP is $800 to $1,200 million.

Illustration 34

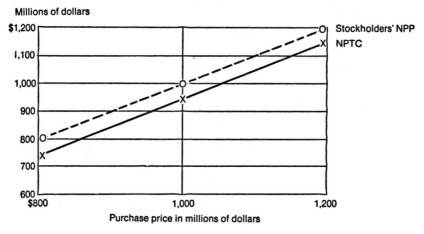

TYPE B REORGANIZATION

**Net Present Tax Cost (NPTC) to XYZ Corporation versus
Net Present Proceeds (NPP) to ABC's Stockholders**

5.8 TYPE C REORGANIZATION

If a Type C Reorganization is contemplated, we will assume that XYZ Corporation will purchase in a Subsidiary Stock for Assets Exchange all the assets and assume the stated liabilities of ABC in exchange solely for voting stock of XYZ. ABC Corporation will distribute all of the XYZ stock received to its stockholders as part of the transaction.

5.801   NPTC

In this case the NPTC will mirror the cost in the Type B Reorganization. XYZ's NPTC will range between $745 and $1,145 million (see Illustration 35).

Illustration 35
Type C Reorganization—Calculation of NPTC *(In Millions)*

Purchase Price	$800	$1,000	$1,200
Less: Present value of tax savings for depreciable assets	55	55	55
NPTC	$745	$ 945	$1,145

5.802   NPP

Given that ABC exchanged its assets and liabilities solely for XYZ's stock, the NPP would be the same as under a Type B Reorganization (see Illustration 36).

The NPP would change if the target's shareholders received any boot in the transaction or if they intend to liquidate the stockholdings of XYZ in the future. We will again note that the target company's shareholders are assuming the risk associated with holding the acquiring company's stock.

Illustration 36
Type C Reorganization—Calculation of NPP to ABC's Stockholders
(In Millions)

Selling Price	$800	$1,000	$1,200
NPP	$800	$1,000	$1,200

5.803   Presentation of Results

The analysis for a Type C Reorganization is graphed in Illustration 37. XYZ's NPTC is between $745 and $1,145 million while ABC or its shareholders' NPP is $800 to $1,200 million.

Illustration 37

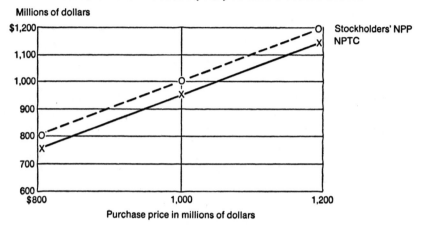

TYPE C REORGANIZATION

**Net Present Tax Cost (NPTC) to XYZ Corporation versus
Net Present Proceeds (NPP) to ABC's Stockholders**

Millions of dollars

Purchase price in millions of dollars

5.9 RESULTS OF COMPARATIVE ANALYSIS

The goal of the comparative approach described in this chapter is to provide useful information for the decision maker on the real cost of effecting a transaction under different acquisition methods. The graphs appearing in the illustrations at the end of each analysis of the sample problem assist the decision maker somewhat towards this goal. They display the NPTC for XYZ Corporation and the NPP for ABC's stockholders under each method. However, what the decision maker really needs to see is (1) a comparative analysis of the NPTC to XYZ under the various methods and (2) a comparative analysis of the NPP to ABC's stockholders under the various methods. These graphs are shown in Illustrations 38 and 39. Why are these graphs useful? First, the NPTC comparative analysis indicates to the decision maker what type of acquisition method would be the least costly under all purchase prices being considered. Second, it permits the decision maker to easily compare costs assuming different purchase prices and acquisition methods. For example, the NPTC comparative analysis graph in Illustration 38 indicates that the NPTC for an Asset Acquisition assuming a $1,200 million purchase price is approximately $950 million. The real cost of any other type of transaction would be about the same even if the "purchase price" is $200 million lower. Third, the NPTC comparative analy-

Illustration 38

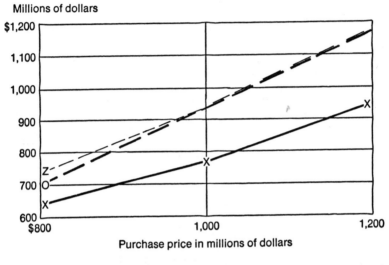

COMPARATIVE ANALYSIS

**Net Present Tax Cost (NPTC) to XYZ Corporation
under the Six Alternate Acquisition Methods**

Millions of dollars

Purchase price in millions of dollars

X = Asset acquisition   O = 338 transaction   Z = All other methods

sis indicates whether the acquiring company should lean towards a 338
Transaction rather than a Stock Acquisition. Fourth, the NPP comparative analysis (Illustration 39) indicates what type of acquisition method
the target company's shareholders will prefer under any purchase price
being considered, all other things being equal. Fifth, the NPP comparative analysis graph allows the decision maker to understand the trade-
offs that the target's shareholders are facing. Assuming that they do not
want a nontaxable transaction (an A, B, or C Reorganization), they will
attempt to negotiate the transaction as a Stock Acquisition or a 338
Transaction because the NPP under these methods clearly exceeds the
NPP in an Asset Acquisition. How much is a Stock Acquisition or 338
Transaction worth to them? It is apparent from the graph that a Stock
Acquisition or 338 Transaction at any price generates NPPs that approximate the NPPs from an Asset Acquisition completed at a purchase
price approximately $180–$190 million larger.

Illustration 39

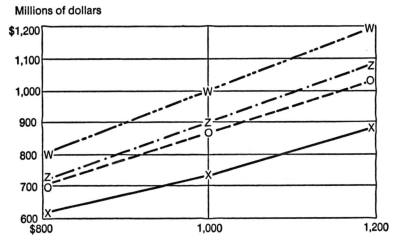

| COMPARATIVE ANALYSIS |

Net Present Tax Proceeds (NPP) to ABC Corporation's Stockholders under the Six Alternate Acquisition Methods

Millions of dollars

Purchase price in millions of dollars

X = Asset Acquisition   O = 338 Transaction and
                                                Stock Acquisition

Z = Type A Reorganization   W = Type B and C Reorganizations

SECTION TWO COST ANALYSIS CONCLUSION

Chapter 1 indicated that the objective of the Cost Section was to answer the question "What will an acquisition cost?" It should be clear by now that the cost of an acquisition depends heavily on the acquisition method used to effect the transaction. Therefore, the best answer we could give the decision maker is an analysis for understanding cost in the context of different methods and purchase prices. In laying the foundation for this analysis we reviewed some fundamental concepts of acquisition cost, the alternate acquisition methods that can be used to effect a transaction, a theoretical framework for calculating the real economic cost and proceeds in a transaction, and the nontax factors that influence the buyer and seller. The culmination of this section was Chapter 5 wherein the analytical approach for comparing the costs and proceeds under different acquisition methods and purchase prices was proposed.

REFERENCES FOR SECTION TWO

Acquisitions and Mergers Tactics and Techniques 1983, 189–226. New York: Practicing Law Institute, 1983.

Bittker, Boris I, and James S. Eustice. *Federal Income Taxation of Corporations and Shareholders,* 4th ed., chap. 14. Boston, Mass.: Warren, Gorham & Lamont, 1979.

Bradley, James W., and Donald H. Korn. *Acquisition and Corporate Development,* 165, 184. Lexington, Mass: Lexington Books, 1981.

Depreciation Guide. Chicago: Commerce Clearing House, 1981.

Eustice, James S. *Federal Income Taxation of Corporations and Shareholders 1984 Cumulative Supplement No. 1,* chap. 14. Boston, Mass.: Warren, Gorham & Lamont, 1984.

Fox, B. *Corporate Acquisitions and Mergers,* chaps. 2–5, 23–26. New York: Matthew Bender & Co., 1979.

Freund, James C. *Anatomy of a Merger.* New York: Law Journal Press, 1975.

Herz, John W., and Charles H. Ballar, ed. *Business Acquisitions,* 2d ed., chaps. 8, 12, 22, 28. New York: Practicing Law Institute, 1981.

Scharf, Charles A. *Acquisitions, Mergers, Sales and Takeovers,* chaps. 10, 11. Englewood Cliffs, N. J.: Prentice-Hall, 1979.

Tufts, *The Taxable Merger,* 7 J. Corp. Tax 342 (1981).

1984 U.S. Master Tax Guide. Chicago: Commerce Clearing House, 1983.

Section Three

Risk and Return Analysis

Introduction

Section Three addresses the questions of risk and return. The risk and return analysis proposed in the section's sole chapter involves (1) developing a cash flow model for the target, including all the tax considerations identified in Section Two, (2) making alternate operating scenario assumptions (Best Case, Most Likely Case, and Worst Case); (3) performing sensitivity analyses on the key operating variables; and (4) determining the internal rate of return (IRR) on the acquisition's cash flows under the different operating scenarios and purchase prices. An acquisition's IRR is calculated rather than its net present value because the key to successful negotiations is giving the chief negotiator (who is often not a financial person) as much information as possible about the transaction in a highly intelligible form, and the IRR method results in a percentage figure that most executives readily understand. The end result of the risk and return analysis is a matrix of rates of return that the acquiring company can expect given the spectrum of likely purchase prices. The author believes this is the best answer one can give top management concerning the risk and return queries. The final step required in analyzing an acquisition is to determine the impact that the acquisition will have on the acquiring company.

Chapter 6

The Acquisition Model

6.1 INTRODUCTION

Thus far in the 1980s there has been a great deal of merger and acquisition activity that has been motivated by a philosophy of "corporate restructuring" to reflect a focused strategic direction. However, despite this zeal for strategic repositioning, many acquisitions fail to create value for the acquiring company's shareholders because management overpays for the cash flow stream that the target can reasonably be expected to generate. Minimizing this risk can best be accomplished by a detailed financial evaluation of the target company. The primary purpose of this chapter is to describe how such a detailed **discounted cash flow (DCF)** evaluation of a target company can be performed. The objective in preparing this analysis is to obtain the most realistic estimate of the cash flows that can be expected as a result of the acquisition and indicate how the results of the financial analysis can be exhibited to aid the top management of the acquiring company make the pricing decision on the target and formulate their negotiating strategy. Furthermore, in an effort to aid the decision makers evaluate the riskiness of the acquisition, various operating scenarios must be devised and sensitivity analysis performed on the key operating variables. Finally, the impact of the acquisition on the acquiring company must be analyzed.

In attempting to prepare cash flow estimates, one is confronted with the problem that executives generally use and understand financial statements prepared on the basis of **generally accepted accounting principles (GAAP),** not statements prepared solely on the basis of cash flows. The approach taken here to circumvent this problem is to prepare a forecast that is primarily cash flow oriented but that incorporates an income statement prepared on a basis that closely resembles a GAAP income statement. The rationale for taking this approach is that preparing an income statement on a GAAP basis will heighten management's level of comfort with the projections.

One of the principle factors that dictate the need for a detailed analysis of an acquisition is the U.S. tax law. As we have seen in Section Two, tax considerations can so significantly affect cash flows that they must be incorporated into any realistic analysis.

6.2   CRITICAL INFORMATION SOUGHT

Management in performing a financial evaluation of an acquisition candidate is looking for an answer to the query "What is this company worth?" Theoretically, a target company is worth an amount equal to the value of all future cash flows it is expected to generate, discounted at a rate agreed upon by management of the acquiring company. Practically speaking, this definition is deficient because it does not reveal the relationship between future cash flows and the purchase price that exists as a result of U.S. tax laws concerning depreciation of fixed assets and amortization of goodwill. Generally, a company's expected cash flow cannot be computed without taking into consideration the purchase price because the purchase price dictates the depreciation deductions that the company will be able to claim for tax purposes. Furthermore, to the extent that the purchase price includes an amount paid for goodwill, as opposed to depreciable assets, cash flow will be negatively influenced because goodwill cannot be deducted for tax purposes. Therefore, the worth of a company depends in part on its purchase price. Given this circumstance, the best answer that a financial department can give top management as to the worth of a company is a range of after-tax returns that the acquirer can expect given the spectrum of likely purchase prices.

Companies are often faced with potential acquisition candidates that are operating in the same or closely related fields. In such cases incremental revenues or cost savings (synergies) are generally expected.[1] As a rule acquiring companies do not want to pay for the value associated with the synergy to be realized. Unfortunately, many times the company to be acquired has sought out the acquiring company precisely because of the value of the incremental revenues or cost savings that will result from the combination of the two companies. In these instances it is unlikely that the acquiring company will be able to consummate a purchase at a price that does not include some value for the expected incremental revenues or cost savings. The financial department of the acquiring company needs to provide two after-tax return analyses in these situations—one including and one excluding all synergies. Management needs the "before-synergies" analysis to decide on an opening bid. The "after-synergies" analysis allows management to determine how much of the value associated with the realization of the incremental revenues or cost savings they can afford to pay the acquired company's owners (e.g., shareholders or parent company) and still meet their targeted after-tax return on investment objective.

6.3   KEY DECISION BY TOP MANAGEMENT

Concurrent with the determination of the range of after-tax returns available, top management must define the minimum return level it seeks in making this particular acquisition.[2] This determination hinges on management's estimation of the risk associated with the company to be acquired. The more speculative the investment, the higher the minimum return management will require. The minimum return acceptable to management will determine the maximum price the acquiring company should be willing to pay.

6.4   ALTERNATE ACQUISITION METHODS CONSIDERED

Chapter 3 was devoted to analyzing the various acquisition methods. In building the cash flow forecast for the target company, alternate models should be developed for each acquisition method that is being considered. These models should incorporate the cash flows associated with each particular acquisition method. In paragraph 4.201 we discounted the cash flows from tax savings at a rate slightly in excess of the Treasury bill rate in calculating the Net Present Tax Cost (NPTC) for the buyer. Here we will merely include the expected cash flows from the tax savings with the other cash flows of the acquisition in determining the project's internal rate of return. The rationale for this approach is that we do not want to distinguish among the factors contributing to the acquisition's total expected cash flows based on their risk. We are looking for a composite internal rate of return for the entire project.

6.5   ASSUMPTIONS USED IN CREATING CASH FLOWS

To date many financial departments have used relatively simple cash flow models to value acquisitions. In these models only five or six general assumptions are needed to generate a projected cash flow stream. The cash flow formula for one of these models appears below:[3]

$$CF_t = S_{t-1}(1 + g_t)(p_t)(1-T_t) - (S_t - S_{t-1})(f_t + W_t)$$

where:

CF = cash flow
S = sales
g = annual growth rate in sales
p = EBIT as a percentage of sales
T = income tax rate
f = capital investment required (i.e., total capital investment net of replacement of existing capacity estimated by depreciation) per dollar of sales increase
W = cash required for net working capital per dollar of sales increase
t = time period

The major problem with these models is that the variables used to estimate the cash flow stream are so unlike the concepts that management deals with on a continuing basis that the results have to be suspect. For instance, estimating the capital investment per dollar of sales increase would appear particularly difficult. A line manager familiar with the potential acquisition's operation may be able to give a good estimate of the capital required in the future by that company, but he may or may not understand what is meant by the capital investment per dollar of sales increase. Another approach often substituted for line management input is for the financial department to come up with their own estimates of the required coefficients based on historical relationships. However, if the target company is in a fast-changing environment, these are not the type of estimates one would like plugged into the model.

The remainder of this chapter describes an expanded model for estimating the cash flows associated with a prospective acquisition and suggests a method for presenting the results of the analysis. The model combines business concepts that line management should be thoroughly familiar with and financial concepts that are well known by all financial departments. This model is put forth only for illustrative purposes. As will become apparent, the model needs to be tailored to each individual acquisition.

6.6 AN EXPANDED CASH FLOW MODEL

The expanded cash flow model consists of 11 basic schedules including (in order of required preparation):

The information flows required by the model are diagrammed in Illustration 1.

Illustration 1
Diagram of Information Flows in Expanded Cash Flow Model

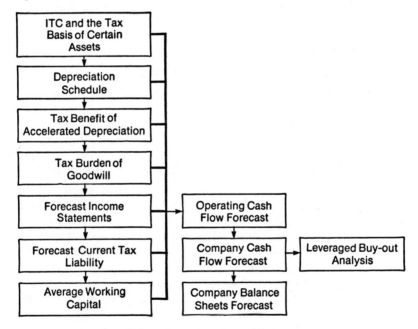

6.601   ITC and the Tax Basis of Certain Assets

The primary purpose of this schedule is to generate an estimate of the tax credits that will be available to the company (see paragraph B.504

for a discussion of the tax credits available on the purchase of used Section 38 property). The data required to generate this schedule includes capital expenditures over the time horizon of the analysis, an estimate of the percentage of expenditures qualifying for tax credits, and a forecast of the tax credit rate. In arriving at the last two assumptions, consultations should be held with the corporation's tax manager or independent public accounting firm. In these discussions the nature of the anticipated capital expenditures should be reviewed so that the tax manager or independent public accounting firm can determine whether the expenditures will qualify for any tax credits.

A second objective of this schedule is to compute the tax basis of certain assets that generate tax credits. Generally the basis of such assets must be reduced by one half the amount of such credits. This reduced adjusted basis will be used to determine both cost recovery deductions and gain or loss when the asset is sold or exchanged (see paragraphs B.401b and B.507). Instead of reducing an asset's basis, a taxpayer may alternatively elect to reduce the regular investment tax credit by 2 percent as described in paragraph B.507.

This schedule must be prepared first because the tax basis of assets are required inputs to the Depreciation Schedule.

6.602   Depreciation Schedule

The purpose of the Depreciation Schedule is to calculate book and tax depreciation and amortization. The purchase price for any company can be conceived of as having two components: a working capital component and the remainder. The remainder consists of the value paid for net plant, goodwill, intangible assets, and other assets. In order to compute the depreciation and amortization deductions, this remainder must be allocated to the various fixed asset accounts, intangible assets, and goodwill. The allocations of value for book purposes and tax purposes may differ (see discussion in paragraph C.202). Furthermore, in acquisitions to be consummated under a No Change in Basis Acquisition Method, the acquiring company will merely inherit the adjusted tax basis and tax depreciation methods for the target company's assets. For acquisitions where the acquiring company will obtain a new cost basis in the target company's assets, the allocation of the remainder to various asset accounts is difficult, especially early in the evaluation process. However, to the extent that line management is familiar with the acquisition candidate's operations and is able to provide the necessary assumptions these difficulties are eased. The allocation process must be accomplished keeping in mind that the seller in an asset deal will have a strong point of view on how such allocations should be done; the seller's primary interest being the minimization of any recapture liability.

Furthermore, the allocations must be performed in a reasonable manner to prevent the IRS from changing it and ultimately denying deductions. The rules for allocating value to asset categories are reviewed for tax purposes in paragraph 3.203 and for book purposes in Appendix C. The allocations should be based on consistent assumptions as to the fair market value of assets in both analyses.

Another required input for the Depreciation Schedule is a forecast of the capital expenditures by the various asset categories over the horizon of the analysis. A key point here is that if a major capital spending program to reduce costs is anticipated, the concurrent savings should be built into the income statement later.

In calculating the tax depreciation on the target company's assets in New Cost Basis Acquisitions, the ACRS statutory percentages are used (see paragraph B.401b). Other assumptions required to generate the schedule include the company's "book" depreciation and amortization methods and useful lives for various asset categories and an estimate of what the "marginal" combined federal, state, and local income tax rate would be for the acquired company excluding any tax benefits such as investment credits or accelerated depreciation.

6.603   Tax Benefit of Accelerated Depreciation

This schedule will calculate the tax benefit or burden of accelerated depreciation to the acquiring company based on the book and tax depreciation figures generated in the prior schedule. See paragraph 6.606 for a discussion of why this benefit is separately calculated.

6.604   Tax Burden of Goodwill

This schedule will calculate the tax burden associated with any goodwill (see paragraph 3.403c) based on the amortization figures calculated in the Depreciation Schedule. See paragraph 6.606 for a discussion of why this burden is separately calculated.

6.605   Forecast Income Statements

One of the most significant advantages of the expanded model is that a full income statement with supporting assumptions is prepared. For instance, with a five- or six-variable model it is difficult to say exactly what level of sales volume or pricing is assumed for key product lines. In the expanded model these assumptions must be explicitly stated in order to generate a result. Given the nature of these assumptions, management of the acquiring company can heighten their level of comfort with the results of the evaluation.

The income statement should be constructed in a manner that conforms closely to GAAP. This approach is desirable because executives are familiar with reviewing income statements prepared on this basis. The exception to this general rule is that cost of goods sold should be estimated exclusive of any depreciation and amortization expenses. Such costs should be treated as a separate line item on the income statement. Other assumptions required to generate the income statement include major product line volumes and prices, and the level of selling, general, and administrative costs (excluding depreciation or amortization) over the horizon of the analysis.

One of the key problems in constructing an income statement is dealing with the inventory costing method used. Two of the most widely used methods are the first-in, first-out (FIFO) method and the last- in, first out (LIFO) method. Both are acceptable under generally accepted accounting principles. Accounting for cost of goods sold under the FIFO method is based on the assumption that the goods first produced are the goods first sold. This concept approximates the physical flow of inventories in most companies. A result of the FIFO approach is that inventory on hand at the end of any period is priced at the latest cost. In times of inflation, companies using the FIFO method will report higher earnings than one's using LIFO. Accounting for the cost of goods sold under LIFO method is based on the assumption that operations require a certain minimum quantity of inventory and that increases in the value of that inventory should not be reflected in income. The costs of goods sold are determined at the latest costs and inventory is priced at the earliest cost. The prime reasons motivating many companies to switch from FIFO to LIFO over the last decade are that LIFO (1) provides a better matching of sales with the cost of those sales and (2) indefinitely defers the payment of income taxes on increases in year-end inventory values. The most significant deterrent to adopting LIFO is that the IRS requires LIFO to be used for financial reporting purposes if it is to be utilized for tax purposes. In a period of substantial inflation the tax deferrals can significantly impact cash flows. However, adopting LIFO in such an environment will significantly lower reported earnings. The model uses a simple approach to the problem wherein the cost of goods sold percentage for each year is judgmentally estimated keeping in mind the costing method utilized. This approach will result in different gross profit percentages depending upon whether the company uses FIFO or LIFO. Note that in either case the cost of goods sold is estimated exclusive of any depreciation or amortization expenses. If the target company is using FIFO and continued inflation and stable inventory unit levels are expected, a higher gross profit percentage should be forecast than if the company were using LIFO. Generally, where inventory levels and the product mix are expected to remain relatively constant, this approach is adequate. If this is not the case, a more complex system for estimating the cost of goods sold may be required.

The income statement described above provides for only a few captions: Sales, Cost of Goods Sold, Selling, General and Administrative Expenses, and Operating Profit. This limited detail can be expanded to include any number of major cost captions. Such detail can be prepared on separate schedules with total figures carried up to the abbreviated income statement or broken out right in the income statement itself. Furthermore, one can link particular cost components to assumed sales volumes.

The income statement contains sales and operating profit data that are essential inputs for the Current Tax Liability schedule and the Forecast Average Working Capital schedule.

6.606 Current Tax Liability

One of the more difficult figures to estimate in the expanded model is the target's average current income tax liability over the course of a year. The current year's tax liability is a function of its taxable income; capital gains and losses: federal, state, and local tax rates; the company's minimum tax; and any tax credits the company has earned. We will assume in calculating the current tax liability that there are no capital gains or losses, that the marginal combined federal, state, and local income tax rate is 50 percent, and that there is no tax burden associated with the minimum tax rules or the corporate tax preference cut back (but see paragraph B.9).

The approach taken in calculating the current income tax liability is to segregate the key components of taxable income. Taxable income is composed of the company's book operating profit adjusted for the effects of permanent and timing differences between pretax accounting income and taxable income. Permanent differences between pretax accounting income and taxable income involve items that will never reverse at any time. For example, under present tax laws, goodwill cannot be amortized for tax purposes; yet under generally accepted accounting principles, goodwill is to be amortized over a period not to exceed 40 years for book purposes. Timing differences involve those items that affect taxable income in periods different from those in which they affect book income. For example, assets can be depreciated for tax purposes under ACRS much more rapidly than they can for book purposes. This gives rise to a timing difference that provides additional cash flow in the years immediately following the acquisition. This situation reverses itself at the point where book depreciation exceeds tax depreciation. The author believes that it is very worthwhile to understand the cash flow implications of the permanent and timing differences between pretax accounting income and taxable income. Therefore, the tax liability associated with each of the permanent and timing differences is separately calculated in the model.

EXAMPLE 6A   *ABC Corporation has pretax accounting income of $100. In arriving at that figure, ABC Corporation deducted $10 for the amortization of goodwill. Furthermore, ABC Corporation has invested in equipment during the year so it is entitled to take an investment tax credit of $7. Finally, ABC Corporation depreciates its plant and equipment for tax purposes on an accelerated basis using ACRS percentages. The excess of tax depreciation over book depreciation amounts to $20. What is ABC's current tax liability? Both the traditional approach and the approach which segregates the various components appear below.*

Traditional Approach

Pretax accounting income	$100
Less: Accelerated depreciation	(20)
Plus: Goodwill	10
Taxable income	90
Assumed tax rate	50%
Tax	45
Less: Investment tax credits	7
Current tax liability	$ 38

Component Approach

	Pretax Accounting Income	(Par. 6.603) Accelerated Depreciation	(Par. 6.604) Goodwill	Total
	$100	$(20)	$10	$90
Assumed tax rate	50%	50%	50%	50%
Tax effect	$ 50	$(10)	$ 5	$45
Investment tax credits				(7)
Current income tax liability				$38

When viewed using this approach, we see that the company receives a cash flow benefit of $10 due to the fact that it takes accelerated depreciation but pays a penalty of $5 because goodwill cannot be deducted for tax purposes. Throughout the book we refer to this as the Tax Benefit of Accelerated Depreciation and the Tax Burden of Goodwill.

Once the current year's tax liability is calculated, a formula must be devised to convert this figure into an average tax liability estimate. This formula can vary significantly from company to company depending on the seasonality of earnings. We will assume that the company earns income evenly throughout the year and that no estimated quarterly payments are made. See paragraph B.10 for a discussion of the quarterly payment rules. Therefore, the average current income tax liability will equal one half the current income tax liability.

6.607 Forecast Average Working Capital

The Forecast Average Working Capital schedule is designed to calculate the increase or decrease in working capital from year to year for the period under evaluation. The calculation involves estimating the major working capital components: receivables, inventory, prepaid expenses, accounts payable and accrued expenses, and the average income tax liability. The last figure—average income tax liability—is merely transposed from the prior schedule. It is not the purpose of the schedule to estimate the above working capital components as they would be computed under generally accepted accounting principles at a particular point in time. Rather, the schedule is intended to calculate the average amount of funds tied up in each working capital component in current dollars each year.

Receivables generally are a function of sales. Therefore, the average outstanding receivables can be obtained by multiplying net sales times the number of days receivables are anticipated to be outstanding and dividing by 365 days. Generally, whether a company uses FIFO or LIFO significantly affects the inventory figure for balance sheet reporting purposes. However, since the intent of this schedule is to calculate the average inventory investment in current dollars each year, the method of calculating inventories for balance sheet purposes under generally accepted accounting principles will be disregarded. Average inventory will be calculated as a function of the current cost of goods sold (exclusive of depreciation) and the number of times inventory turns over. Prepaid expenses are estimated as a percentage of total costs (excluding depreciation) or as a percentage of sales. Finally, accounts payable and accrued expenses are a function of cost of goods sold and selling, general, and administrative expenses (both exclusive of depreciation and amortization). Generally, payments for the cost of materials are made on a different time basis than payments for selling, general, and administrative expenses (e.g., materials may have to be paid for in 10 days versus 30 days for selling, general, and administrative type expenses). Thus, the formula for computing the average level of accounts payable and accrued expenses will look like this:

(Cost of goods sold/Number of payments during year)
+ (Selling, general, and administrative expenses/Number
of payments during year)

with the number of payments differing between the two items. The financial department should be able to estimate these figures.

Once an average working capital is calculated, the prior year's figure can be subtracted from it to arrive at the increase or decrease in working capital.

6.608   Operating Cash Flow Forecast

There are two cash flow schedules that are included as part of the acquisition model. They are the Operating Cash Flow Forecast and the Company Cash Flow Forecast. Each serves a different purpose. The Operating Cash Flow Forecast is introduced to analyze the cash flows associated with the acquisition, exclusive of financing. The internal rate of return for the acquisition is calculated based on the operating cash flows, and the author believes that the decision whether or not to effect the transaction should be based on this return. The Company Cash Flow Forecast is provided in order to understand the acquisition's cash flows given a certain method of financing. It should be noted that this information is typically used by **leveraged buy-out (LBO)** investors to make the decision on whether or not to attempt to effect a transaction (see paragraph 6.610). The Company Cash Flow Forecast also provides the necessary interface with the Company Balance Sheets Forecast.

In recent years a number of alternative approaches have been advocated concerning the proper presentation of financing associated with a transaction.[4] The approach advocated here is to exclude financing from the acquisition's cash flow analysis for purposes of making a go/no go decision. This approach enables management to focus exclusively on the profitability of the business to be acquired. Furthermore, it lends itself to overlaying a number of different financing alternatives on the cash flows of the business. Even if a proposed acquisition requires certain financing (e.g., takeover of a company's existing debt obligations or complicated leveraged buy-out financing), the acquirer should go through the process of analyzing the underlying business before it considers the financing aspects of the proposed transaction.

The Operating Cash Flow Forecast summarizes the acquisition's cash flows taking necessary elements from other schedules. The acquisition's operating profit is taken from the Forecast Income Statements schedule; depreciation, amortization, and capital expenditures from the Depreciation Schedule; the Tax Burden of Goodwill and the Tax Benefit of Accelerated Depreciation from their respective schedules; the increase (decrease) in working capital from the Average Working Capital Schedule, and, finally, investment tax credits from the ITC and Tax Basis of Certain Assets schedule.

The remaining items affecting the Operating Cash Flow Forecast schedule involve the residual value of the business and the cash flows from operating synergies. The latter item applies only if synergy will be realized from the acquisition. If such incremental revenues or cost savings will be realized, these items should be separately modeled with the total net cash flow brought forward to the Operating Cash Flow Forecast schedule.

The residual value of the business presents a special problem.[5] Theoretically, the residual value of a business is equal to the present value of the cash flows expected from the business commencing one year after the horizon date of the analysis and continuing in perpetuity. In reality this offers no real guidance for the financial department because their crystal ball cannot be that clear past the horizon of the current analysis. There are a number of alternatives that one can take. Some examples include: *(a)* assign a value to the business equal to its ending net working capital, *(b)* say the company is worth its book value at the end of the period, or *(c)* assign a value equal to an estimated market value for the company. Obviously, there are a number of intermediate positions one can advocate. Therefore, when the financial department performs sensitivity analyses on the proposed acquisition, alternate assumptions should be made about the residual value.

6.609   Company Cash Flow Forecast

The Company Cash Flow Forecast adds the cash flows associated with financing the acquisition to the Operating Cash Flow Forecast. For instance, interest expense on debt, interest income on free cash balances, and the related tax provision on net interest income or expense are included in the schedule. The schedule also provides an opportunity to show payment of dividends, borrowing, repayment of borrowings, and proceeds from equity offerings in the company's cash flows. The addition of the financing aspects of the transaction enables the project's cash flow forecast to integrate with the Company Balance Sheets Forecast.

6.610   Leveraged Buy-Out Analysis

Although the decision to effect a transaction should be based on the internal rate of return associated with the Operating Cash Flow Forecast, the approach taken by certain LBO investors in analyzing proposed transactions should be understood. LBO investors look at three things in determining if a transaction is financially attractive: (1) the size and stability of the Operating Cash Flow Forecast, (2) the amount of the equity investment that they will have to make, and (3) the after-tax cost of the interest and/or preferred stock dividends associated with the financing that will be used. Generally the LBO investor's time horizon on a transaction is much shorter than a typical buyer who is interested in the target company's business. Furthermore, most LBO investors do not expect to realize significant cash flows for themselves until they sell the company. Therefore, the residual value in the Operating Cash Flow Forecast takes on a great deal more importance for the LBO investor.

The Leveraged Buy-Out Analysis schedule should accumulate the three items of information mentioned above and calculate an internal rate of return on the LBO investors equity investment.

6.611 Company Balance Sheets Forecast

Balance sheets for the acquisition are prepared for two reasons: (1) to understand the liquidity and debt financing position of the target in the hands of the acquirer and (2) to overlay the target's balance sheet on the acquirer's own forecast balance sheets so that management can understand the impact of the acquisition on the acquirer's liquidity and debt financing position.

6.7 EVALUATING RISK IN AN ACQUISITION

Thus far the chapter has described a model for calculating the returns available to the acquiring company assuming various purchase prices. Presumably the acquiring company would use its "Most Likely" estimates for all the variables in the model in calculating the returns. However, when the analysis is completed, do we really have enough data to make a decision? Probably not. Why? Each of the variables in the model (e.g., sales volumes, pricing, margins, costs, etc.) has its own range of possible values and probability distribution as to their occurrence. How can we incorporate this fact into our analysis?

6.701 Scenario and Sensitivity Analysis

Scenario and sensitivity analysis are the most useful techniques for revealing the risk inherent in an acquisition. **Scenario analysis** involves developing Best Case, Worst Case, and Most Likely Case operating scenarios for a proposed acquisition. What is an operating scenario? It is a set of assumptions concerning selling prices, volumes, costs, and so forth, that the decision maker believes is representative of what could happen in the Worst Case, Best Case, or Most Likely Case. The technique does not attempt to define the probability of occurrence of either the variables or the operating scenario. The probability of the operating scenario occurring is subjectively determined by the decision maker.

Sensitivity analysis indicates to the decision maker how sensitive the projects returns are to variances from expected values of the key variables. For example, in a given project one might do a sensitivity analysis on selling prices assuming they are 10 percent, 15 percent, and 20 percent higher and lower than expected. Sensitivity analysis does not tell the decision maker anything about the probability of occurrence of a particular value for a variable.

6.701a Example of Sensitivity Analysis

The concept of sensitivity analysis is to adjust key variables from their expected values in the Most Likely Case. This analysis can be done assuming one purchase price or it can be done for all purchase prices analyzed. For example, what effect would a 1 percent, 2 percent, or 3 percent shift in the gross margin percentage have on the projects returns? An example of a matrix of returns resulting from performing such a sensitivity analysis is given in Illustration 2. This matrix is converted to graphic form in Illustration 3.

Illustration 2
Internal Rates of Return Available on Proposed Acquisition Assuming Various Gross Margin Percentages

Gross Margin Percentage	*Purchase Prices*		
	$X	*$X + 1*	*$X + 2*
+ 3	29%	27%	25%
+ 2	24	22	20
+ 1	19	16	14
Most Likely Case	14	12	10
− 1	11	8	6
− 2	5	2	0
− 3	0	−4	−7

Illustration 3
Internal Rates of Return Available on Proposed Project Assuming Various Gross Margin Percentages

Purchase price in thousands of dollars

6.8 PRESENTATION OF RESULTS

The best answer that one can give top management as to the risk and returns associated with a proposed acquisition is a range of after-tax returns that the acquirer can expect given the spectrum of likely purchase prices and operating scenarios. An illustrative matrix is given in Illustration 4. This matrix is converted to a graph in Illustration 5. This graph clearly displays the trade-offs between returns available and purchase price given different operating scenarios.

Illustration 4
Internal Rates of Return Available on Proposed Acquisition

	Purchase Prices		
	$X	*$X + 1*	*$X + 2*
Best Case	16%	14%	12%
Most Likely Case	14	12	10
Worst Case	12	10	8

Illustration 5
Internal Rates of Return Available on Proposed Project

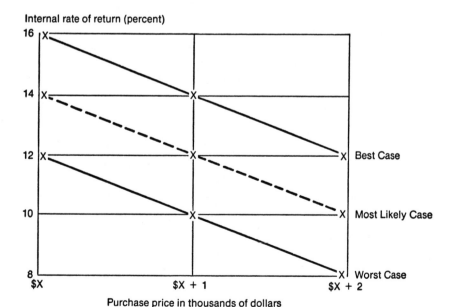

Purchase price in thousands of dollars

6.9   IMPACT ON THE ACQUIRING COMPANY

Assuming that the cash flow model has been completed and the risk analysis performed, the only remaining task is to analyze the effect of the transaction on the acquiring company. The purpose of this analysis is to understand the transaction's impact on the acquiring company's (1) earnings or earnings per share, (2) liquidity, and (3) overall financial structure (e.g., whether the acquisition will give rise to a change in the rating of the acquiring company's outstanding securities). The analysis is performed by consolidating the target company's forecast balance sheets, income statements, and cash flow statements with the acquiring company's forecast statements.

NOTES TO CHAPTER 6

[1]For a complete discussion of how to create value with acquisitions, see Malcolm S. Salter and Wolf A. Weinhold, "Diversification via Acquisition: Creating Value," *Harvard Business Review,* July–August 1978, p. 166.

[2]Alfred Rappaport argues that the minimum return should equal the risk and adjusted cost of capital, "Strategic Analysis for More Profitable Acquisitions," *Harvard Business Review,* July–August 1979, pp. 105–6.

[3]Alfred Rappaport, "Strategic Analysis for More Profitable Acquisitions," *Harvard Business Review,* July–August 1979, p. 103.

[4]For a summarized discussion of these alternative approaches, see Eugene F. Brigham, *Financial Management Theory and Practice,* 2d. ed. (Hinsdale, Ill.: The Dryden Press, 1979), pp. 397–402.

[5]For a discussion of residual value, see M. G. Wright, *Discounted Cash Flow,* 2d ed. (Maidenhead, England: McGraw-Hill Book Company (U.K.) Ltd., 1973), pp. 58–61.

SECTION THREE
RISK AND RETURN ANALYSIS CONCLUSION

Chapter 6 set out the analytical approach for calculating a proposed acquisition's investment returns. This involved building a cash flow model that incorporated all the tax considerations described in Section Two as well as forecast operating cash flows. Having built the model, it would be "run" a number of times under various sets of assumptions about key operating variables. Each time the model is run, an internal rate of return is calculated. The end result of the analysis is a matrix of rates of return that can be expected under various operating scenarios and purchase prices. The model would also be used to perform sensitivity analyses on individual operating variables. Finally, the chapter focused on the need to evaluate the impact of the acquisition on the acquiring company.

Section Four

An Example

Chapter 7

Case of Mareight Corporation

7.1 INTRODUCTION

The purpose of this chapter is to analyze in detail a realistic example of an acquisition using the analytical methods described previously in the book.

General Grocery Products, Inc. (General), is a billion dollar multinational food products company that is searching for profitable U.S. businesses that have products General can market through its existing sales force. A prospective target that appears to meet these criteria is Mareight Corporation. Mareight is a wholly owned subsidiary of United Industries, a Fortune 500 conglomerate. The conglomerate has been holding discussions with General concerning the possible sale of Mareight to General. The conglomerate is interested in divesting the subsidiary to help fund its growth plans in another area. It wants all cash from the sale; and therefore only three alternate methods of consummating the transaction need to be analyzed: (1) Asset Acquisition, (2) 338 Transaction, and (3) Stock Acquisition.

As indicated above, General is interested in acquiring Mareight primarily because it fits within its plans for adding grocery product lines that it can sell through its existing sales force. Currently, Mareight uses a direct sales force of 62 people to market its products nationally. General expects to eliminate approximately 20 of Mareight's salespeople. The annual cost of a salesperson in 1984 is estimated to be $38,000, so the expected annual savings from reducing the sales force will be $760,000. Moreover, General expects to reap about $200,000 in cost savings annually due to the fact that Mareight's packaging requirements can be produced at one of General's existing plants. Finally, General anticipates eliminating a substantial amount of Mareight's duplicative administrative expenses. From a detailed report on selling, general, and administrative expenses supplied by Mareight, General has quantified these expenses in thousands of dollars as follows:

	1982	*1983*	*1984E*
Duplicated administrative expenses	$303	$318	$342

Industry unit volumes in Mareight's particular market segments have been declining at a rate of 5 percent over the last five years. Mareight's unit sales in both its product lines have followed the industry trend. However, the company has put through price increases to maintain its operating profit margin, as costs have kept pace with inflation.

Listed below are Mareight's shipments in millions of units and average unit prices for its two brands:

	1982	*1983*	*1984E*
Sales volume (millions of units):			
Product A	225	206	205
Product B	116	108	104
	359	330	309
Selling prices (in dollars):			
Product A	$0.063	$0.065	$0.067
Product B	0.124	0.129	0.136

Although the industry has been declining steadily at 5 percent for 5 years, General's Most Likely Case volume estimates indicate that because the children born in the "baby boom" period are coming of age, demand for the industry's products will decline only at a compound rate of 1.5 percent over the next 10 years. General's Worst Case estimates show a decline at a compound rate of 3 percent and its Best Case estimates are for unit volumes to remain flat.

Sales and profitability for Mareight have been declining somewhat over the last few years. Mareight's balance sheet information, income statements, and selected other data are given in Illustration 1.

Mareight owns two manufacturing facilities and a warehouse that also has office space for all administrative personnel. Currently, the company spends about $200,000 a year on capital replacements and does not anticipate any additional major outlays in the near future.

General's chief economist has forecast a 6 percent inflation rate for all costs related to Mareight's operations over the next 10 years.

Illustration 1

Mareight Corporation
Income Statements
(In Thousands)

	1982	1983	1984E
Gross sales	$28,664	$27,365	$27,808
Freight	804	836	914
Returns	378	323	290
Net sales	27,482	26,206	26,604
Cost of goods sold*	19,409	18,638	18,790
Gross margin	8,073	7,568	7,814
Selling, general and administrative expenses†	3,948	3,891	4,278
Depreciation and amortization‡	455	417	396
Subtotal	4,403	4,308	4,674
Operating profit	$ 3,670	$ 3,260	$ 3,140

1984E—preliminary estimates.
*Inventories accounted for on FIFO basis.
†Figures exclude any allocation of corporate overhead.
‡All depreciation expenses appear below the gross margin line.

December 31 Balance Sheet Information
(In Thousands)

	1982	1983	1984E
Current Assets			
Cash	$ 604	$ 333	$ 712
Accounts receivable	3,620	3076	3,000
Inventories	6,097	6,495	6,750
Prepaid expenses	205	227	250
Total current assets	10,526	10,131	10,712
Current Liabilities			
Notes payable	1,963	1,914	939
Accounts payable and accrued expenses	1,905	1,671	2,000
Income taxes payable	162	125	106
Total current liabilities	4,030	3,710	3,045
Net working capital	6,496	6,421	7,667
Net property, plant and equipment	3,224	2,897	2,500
Other assets	444	459	468
Net assets employed	$10,164	$ 9,777	$10,635

Selected Data

	1982	1983	1984E
Average inventory	$6,475	$6,425	$6,250
Turnover based on cost of goods sold	3.0	2.9	3.0
Average accounts receivable	$3,400	$3,250	$3,100
Number of days' sales	43	43	41

Preliminary negotiations were begun in November 1984 at which time United indicated to General that their asking price was approximately $6 million over book value at the time of closing. We will assume that any transaction would close on January 1, 1985.

Note that Mareight does not have any long-term liabilities that General would have to assume. Furthermore, any cash or notes payable balance would be eliminated prior to the closing.

General anticipates that it would finance the acquisition by purchasing Mareight for cash and then have Mareight borrow $8 million which Mareight would then forward to General to reduce their equity investment.

7.2   COST ANALYSIS

7.201   Introduction

General's first step in analyzing the proposed transaction was to perform the cost analysis. Due to the fact that the parties were unsure as to the method of effecting the transaction, General requested and received the tax information given in Illustration 2.

Illustration 2
Estimated Book Values and Adjusted Tax Basis at December 31, 1984
(In Thousands)

	Gross Book Values	Net Book Values	Adjusted Tax basis
Accounts receivable		$ 3,000	$3,000
Inventory		6,750	6,750
Prepaid expenses		250	250
Accounts payable		(2,000)	(2,000)
Net working capital		8,000	8,000
Property, plant, and equipment:			
Land	$ 50	50	50
Vehicles	80	24	0
Office equipment	120	26	0
Machinery and equipment	2,950	1,439	430
Buildings and improvements	1,800	961	540
Property, plant, and equipment	$5,000	2,500	1,020
Goodwill		0	0
Net assets purchases		$10,500	$9,020

Note: General informed United that it would not purchase any "other assets" that consisted of loans to officers no longer with Mareight and a long-term note receivable.

The investment tax credits taken on machinery and equipment by Mareight are as follows (in thousands):

1978	$ 5.4
1979	6.9
1980	8.0
1981	4.4
1982	10.1
1983	7.8
1984E	3.1

General's cost analysis consisted of analyzing the transaction under three alternate methods: (1) Asset Acquisition, (2) 338 Transaction, and (3) Stock Acquisition. Given that United had stated a purchase price, General decided that a reasonable range of purchase prices to analyze would be $4 million to $6 million over book value excluding certain items, such as cash, other assets, and any notes payable. If United had not specified an asking price, General would have chosen a wider range of purchase prices over which to do their analysis.

7.202   Asset Acquisition

7.202a   Introduction
Having chosen a purchase price range to analyze, General selected $4 million, $5 million, and $6 million over book value, excluding certain items as the specific purchase prices it would analyze. General's financial staff came up with preliminary estimates of fair market values for all Mareight's assets and liabilities for the three selected purchase prices to analyze. Due to the preliminary nature of the estimates, it is reasonable to assume that the fair market values of certain assets—machinery and equipment, buildings and improvements, and goodwill—would rise given a higher purchase price. Why? If a buyer is willing to pay a higher price, this generally indicates that he has higher expectations of the profit potential to be generated by the business' assets. Given this higher profit expectancy, the underlying business assets have more value to him. One might argue that any increase in value over the bottom figures is all attributable to the company's goodwill, but this probably does not reflect reality. Remember, these are preliminary estimates of value, and as such they do not have to be justified to the IRS. If General had hard information (appraisals) available on the fair market values, this information would have been used. Since this was not the case, the allocations given in Illustration 3 were used for both book and tax purposes.

7.202b   NPTC
General's next step was to compute the Net Present Tax Cost (NPTC) under the three purchase prices. In computing the NPTC, General dis-

counted the tax savings associated with the acquisition at 10 percent (see paragraph 4.201). General's calculations regarding depreciation and the related tax savings are given in Illustrations 4–7.

Illustration 3
Allocation of Purchase Price to Asset Categories *(In Thousands)*

	Estimated December 31, 1984 Net Book Values	Purchase Price $14,500	$15,500	$16,500
Accounts receivable	$ 3,000	$ 3,000	$ 3,000	$ 3,000
Inventory	6,750	6,750	6,750	6,750
Prepaid expenses	250	250	250	250
Accounts payable	(2,000)	(2,000)	(2,000)	(2,000)
Net working capital	8,000	8,000	8,000	8,000
Property, plant, and equipment:				
Land	50	250	250	250
Vehicles	24	100	100	100
Office equipment	26	100	100	100
Machinery and equipment	1,439	2,600	3,000	3,300
Buildings and improvements	961	3,400	3,800	4,250
Property, plant, and equipment	2,500	6,450	7,250	8,000
Goodwill	0	50	250	500
Net assets purchased	$10,500	$14,500	$15,500	$16,500

Note: General assumed that since inventories are kept on a FIFO basis, the balance sheet value for inventories approximates their fair market value.

Illustration 4
Calculation of the Net Present Value of the Tax Savings from the Depreciation Deductions for Vehicles *(Dollar Figures in Thousands)*

		$14,500	$15,500	$16,500
Total purchase price		$14,500	$15,500	$16,500
Fair market value of vehicles		100	100	100
	Year			
ACRS depreciation percentages	1	25%	25%	25%
for 3-year class of property	2	38	38	38
	3	37	37	37
Depreciation deductions	1	$ 25	$ 25	$ 25
	2	38	38	38
	3	37	37	37
Tax savings at 50%	1	13	13	13
	2	19	19	19
	3	19	19	19
10% present value factors	1	.9091	.9091	.9091
	2	.8264	.8264	.8264
	3	.7513	.7513	.7513
Present value of tax savings	1	$ 11	$ 11	$ 11
	2	16	16	16
	2	14	14	14
		$ 41	$ 41	$ 41

Illustration 5
Calculation of the Net Present Value of the Tax Savings from the Depreciation Deductions for Office Equipment *(Dollar Figures in Thousands)*

	Year	$14,500	$15,500	$16,500
Total purchase price		$14,500	$15,500	$16,500
Fair market value of office equipment		100	100	100
ACRS depreciation percentages	1	15%	15%	15%
for 5-year class of property	2	22	22	22
	3	21	21	21
	4	21	21	21
	5	21	21	21
Depreciation deductions	1	$ 15	$ 15	$ 15
	2	22	22	22
	3	21	21	21
	4	21	21	21
	5	21	21	21
Tax savings at 50%	1	8	8	8
	2	11	11	11
	3	11	11	11
	4	11	11	11
	5	11	11	11
10% present value factors	1	.9091	.9091	.9091
	2	.8264	.8264	.8264
	3	.7513	.7513	.7513
	4	.6830	.6830	.6830
	5	.6209	.6209	.6209
Present value of tax savings	1	$ 7	$ 7	$ 7
	2	9	9	9
	3	8	8	8
	4	7	7	7
	5	7	7	7
		$ 37	$ 37	$ 37

Having computed the present value of the future tax savings coming from depreciation deductions, General calculated the NPTC under the three purchase prices analyzed (see Illustration 8).

7.202c   NPP

Once the NPTC was computed, General estimated the Net Present Proceeds (NPP) to the seller. The NPP to be received by the seller included the value of all cash and cash equivalents plus the present value of all other forms of consideration less the present value of the tax burden that the seller would bear, either presently or in the future, as a result

Illustration 6
Calculation of the Net Present Value of the Tax Savings from the
Depreciation Deductions for Machinery and Equipment
(Dollar Figures in Thousands)

Total purchase price		$14,500	$15,500	$16,500
Fair market value of machinery and equipment		2,600	3,000	3,300
	Year			
ACRS depreciation percentages	1	15%	15%	15%
for 5-year class of property	2	22	22	22
	3	21	21	21
	4	21	21	21
	5	21	21	21
Depreciation deductions	1	$ 390	$ 450	$ 495
	2	572	660	726
	3	546	630	693
	4	546	630	693
	5	546	630	693
Tax savings at 50%	1	195	225	248
	2	286	330	363
	3	273	315	347
	4	273	315	347
	5	273	315	347
10% present value factors	1	.9091	.9091	.9091
	2	.8264	.8264	.8264
	3	.7513	.7513	.7513
	4	.6830	.6830	.6830
	5	.6209	.6209	.6209
Present value of tax savings	1	$ 177	$ 205	$ 225
	2	236	273	300
	3	205	237	260
	4	186	215	237
	5	170	196	215
		$ 975	$1,125	$1,237

of the transaction. The NPP was relatively easy to calculate because General was able to obtain information from United on the tax basis of Mareight's assets and investment tax credits taken. Therefore, General could identify the amount of depreciation and investment tax credit recapture. In calculating the NPP, General assumed that if the transaction were effected as a straightforward Asset Acquisition, United would liquidate Mareight Corporation in a 337 Liquidation. General estimated that United's tax basis in its investment in Mareight was $9,020,000.

There are two important facts to remember about a 337 Liquidation. First, generally no gains or losses are recognized by the selling corporation if it has adopted a plan of liquidation. Second, the selling cor-

Illustration 7
Calculation of the Net Present Value of the Tax Savings from the Depreciation Deductions for Buildings and Improvements
(Dollar Figures in Thousands)

	Year	$14,500	$15,500	$16,500
Total purchase price		$14,500	$15,500	$16,500
Fair market value of buildings and improvements		3,400	3,800	4,250
ACRS depreciation percentages for 18-year class of property	1	9%	9%	9%
	2	9	9	9
	3	8	8	8
	4	7	7	7
	5	6	6	6
	6	6	6	6
	7	5	5	5
	8	5	5	5
	9	5	5	5
	10	5	5	5
Depreciation deductions	1	$ 306	$ 342	$ 383
	2	306	342	383
	3	272	304	340
	4	238	266	298
	5	204	228	255
	6	204	228	255
	7	170	190	213
	8	170	190	213
	9	170	190	213
	10	170	190	213
Tax savings at 50%	1	153	171	191
	2	153	171	191
	3	136	152	170
	4	119	133	149
	5	102	114	128
	6	102	114	128
	7	85	95	106
	8	85	95	106
	9	85	95	106
	10	85	95	106
10% present value factors	1	.9091	.9091	.9091
	2	.8264	.8264	.8264
	3	.7513	.7513	.7513
	4	.6830	.6830	.6830
	5	.6209	.6209	.6209
	6	.5645	.5645	.5645
	7	.5132	.5132	.5132
	8	.4665	.4665	.4665
	9	.4241	.4241	.4241
	10	.3855	.3855	.3855

Illustration 7 (*concluded*)

	Year			
Total purchase price		$14,500	$15,500	$16,500
Fair market value of buildings and improvements		3,400	3,800	4,250
Present value of tax savings	1	139	155	174
	2	126	141	158
	3	102	114	128
	4	81	91	102
	5	63	71	79
	6	58	64	72
	7	44	49	55
	8	40	44	50
	9	36	40	45
	10	33	37	41
		$ 722	$ 807	$ 902

Illustration 8
Asset Acquisition—Calculation of NPTC *(In Thousands)*

	$14,500	$15,500	$16,500
Purchase price	$14,500	$15,500	$16,500
Less: Present value of tax savings from depreciation deductions for:			
Vehicles	(41)	(41)	(41)
Office equipment	(37)	(37)	(37)
Machinery and equipment	(975)	(1,125)	(1,237)
Buildings and improvements	(722)	(807)	(902)
NPTC	$12,725	$13,490	$14,283

poration will recognize investment credit, LIFO, and depreciation recapture.

The tax burden that United would bear on the sale consisted of the tax on the depreciation and investment tax credits recaptured by Mareight on the disposition of assets and the tax on any gain on the liquidation of Mareight Corporation. Mareight Corporation depreciated all buildings and improvements on a straight-line basis for tax purposes so there was no depreciation recapture related to this asset. Mareight's investment tax credit, depreciation recapture, and Section 1231 gain calculations are given in Illustrations 9 and 10. See paragraph B.405 for a complete discussion of depreciation recapture, paragraph B.304 for a discussion of the interplay of Section 1231 with the depreciation recapture provisions, and paragraph B.508 for a review of the recapture of investment tax credits (ITC). The net results of the calculations are that the estimated ITC recapture is $27,000, the Section 1245 depreciation recapture amounts to between $2,350,000 and $2,700,000, and there is Section 1231 gain of between $20,000 and $370,000.

The Gain on Net Assets Sold schedule calculates the taxable gain at various prices and the character of any gain. Let us review the calculations for the $15.5 million purchase price. Accounts receivable and inventory are purchased at a price equal to their adjusted basis so there is no gain or loss associated with these items. The depreciation recapture and Section 1231 gain amounts associated with vehicles, office equipment, and machinery and equipment have been calculated in the schedule given in Illustration 10 and are merely repeated here for completeness. Land and buildings and improvements are both Section 1231 assets. Therefore, the gain associated with either is Section 1231 income. Note that there is no depreciation recapture associated with the buildings and improvements because these assets were assumed to have been depreciated on a straight-line basis (see paragraph B.405). Goodwill is a capital asset (not a Section 1231 asset) in the hands of the target. Therefore, the gain associated with its sale is capital gain. Finally, there is no taxable gain on the assumption of Mareight's liabilities (see Illustration 11).

Mareight's tax burden is calculated in Illustration 12. This tax burden potentially has three components: (1) the ordinary income tax due on the Section 1245 recapture income (see paragraph B.405), (2) the tax calculated at the capital gains rate on the sum of the Section 1231 gain and any long-term capital gain (see paragraph B.3), and (3) the tax due on the recapture of investment tax credits (see paragraph B.7). Since General assumed that United would liquidate Mareight under Section 337, the tax burden is only the sum of (1) and (3) above, whereas if it did not liquidate, the tax burden would be the sum of all three components.

Illustration 9
Investment Tax Credit Recapture for Machinery and Equipment
(Dollar Figures in Thousands)

Year Placed in Service	Useful Life	Class of Property	ITC Taken	Recapture Percentage	ITC Recapture
1978	7+		$ 5.4	33.3	$ 1.8
1979	7+		6.9	33.3	2.3
1980	7+		8.0	66.6	5.3
1981		5-year	4.4	40.0	1.8
1982		5-year	10.1	60.0	6.1
1983		5-year	7.8	80.0	6.2
1984		5-year	3.1	100.0	3.1
				Total	$26.6
				Say	$27

Illustration 10
Calculation of Section 1245 Depreciation Recapture and Section 1231 Gain *(In Thousands)*

Selling price	$14,500	$15,500	$16,500
Vehicles fair market value	100	100	100
Adjusted basis			
Realized gain	$ 100	$ 100	$ 100
Accumulated depreciation	$ 80	$ 80	$ 80
Section 1245 recapture income*	$ 80	$ 80	$ 80
Section 1231 gain	20	20	20
Recognized gain	$ 100	$ 100	$ 100
Office equipment fair market value	$ 100	$ 100	$ 100
Adjusted basis			
Realized gain	$ 100	$ 100	$ 100
Accumulated depreciation	$ 120	$ 120	$ 120
Section 1245 recapture income*	$ 100	$ 100	$ 100
Section 1231 gain			
Recognized gain	$ 100	$ 100	$ 100
Machinery and equipment fair market value	$ 2,600	$ 3,000	$ 3,300
Adjusted basis	430	430	430
Realized gain	$ 2,170	$ 2,570	$ 2,870
Accumulated depreciation	$ 2,520	$ 2,520	$ 2,520
Section 1245 recapture income*	$ 2,170	$ 2,520	$ 2,520
Section 1231 gain		50	350
Recognized gain	$ 2,170	$ 2,570	$ 2,870
Summary of Section 1245 Income			
Vehicles	$ 80	$ 80	$ 80
Office equipment	100	100	100
Machinery and equipment	2,170	2,520	2,520
Total	$ 2,350	$ 2,700	$ 2,700
Summary of Section 1231 Gain			
Vehicles	$ 20	$ 20	$ 20
Office equipment			
Machinery and equipment		50	350
Total	$ 20	$ 70	$ 370

*Lesser of realized gain or accumulated depreciation.

Illustration 11
Asset Acquisition—Gain On Net Assets Sold (In Thousands)

	(A) Gross Book Value	(B) Accumulated Depreciation	(C) Adjusted Basis (A)–(B)	(D) Fair Market Value	(E) Taxable Gain (D)–(C)	(F) Section 1245 Recapture Income Lesser of (B) or (E)	(G) Section 1231 Income (D)–(F)	(H) Capital Gain
$14,500 Purchase Price							*Character of Gain*	
Accounts receivable	$ 3,000		$3,000	$ 3,000				
Inventory	6,750		6,750	6,750				
Prepaid expenses	250		250	250				
Land	50		50	250	$ 200			$200
Vehicles	80	$ 80		100	100	$ 80	$ 20	
Office equipment	120	120		100	100	100		
Machinery and equipment	2,950	2,520	430	2,600	2,170	2,170		
Buildings and improvements	1,800	1,260	540	3,400	2,860		2,860	
Goodwill				50	50			50
Accounts payable and accrued expenses	(2,000)		(2,000)	(2,000)				
Totals	$13,000	$3,980	$9,020	$14,500	$5,480	$2,350	$2,880	$250

$15,500 Purchase Price

Accounts receivable	$3,000		$3,000	$3,000				
Inventory	6,750		6,750	6,750				
Prepaid expenses	250		250	250				
Land	50		50	250	$200			$200
Vehicles	80	$80		100	100	$80	$20	
Office equipment	120	120		100	100	100		
Machinery and equipment	2,950	2,520	430	3,000	2,570	2,520	50	
Buildings and improvements	1,800	1,260	540	3,800	3,260		3,260	
Goodwill				250	250			250
Accounts payable and accrued expenses	(2,000)		(2,000)	(2,000)				
Totals	$13,000	$3,980	$9,020	$15,500	$6,480	$2,700	$3,330	$450

$16,500 Purchase Price

Accounts receivable	$3,000		$3,000	$3,000				
Inventory	6,750		6,750	6,750				
Prepaid expenses	250		250	250				
Land	50		50	250	$200			$200
Vehicles	80	$80		100	100	$80	$20	
Office equipment	120	120		100	100	100		
Machinery and equipment	2,950	2,520	430	3,300	2,870	2,520	350	
Buildings and improvements	1,800	1,260	540	4,250	3,710		3,710	
Goodwill				500	500			500
Accounts payable and accrued expenses	(2,000)		(2,000)	(2,000)				
Totals	$13,000	$3,980	$9,020	$16,500	$7,480	$2,700	$4,080	$700

Illustration 12
Mareight Corporation's Tax Burden* *(In Thousands)*

Total purchase price	$14,500	$15,500	$16,500
Tax basis of net assets	9,020	9,020	9,020
Taxable gain	$ 5,480	$ 6,480	$ 7,480
Section 1245 recapture income	$ 2,350	$ 2,700	$ 2,700
Assumed tax rate	50%	50%	50%
Tax burden—(1)	$ 1,175	$ 1,350	$ 1,350
Section 1231 gain	$ 2,880	$ 3,330	$ 4,080
Long-term capital gain	250	450	700
Total gain	3,130	3,780	4,780
Capital gains tax rate	28%	28%	28%
Tax burden—(2)	$ 876	$ 1,058	$ 1,338
Recapture of ITC—(3)	$ 27	$ 27	$ 27
Total tax burden—(1) + (3)	$ 1,202	$ 1,377	$ 1,377

*Exclusive of any burden associated with the alternative minimum tax rules and the corporate tax preference cutback. See paragraph B. 9.

Mareight Corporation's Proceeds Available for Distribution are calculated in Illustration 13 under the liquidation assumption. If Mareight liquidates, United will receive between $13,298,000 and $15,123,000 in proceeds.

Assuming Mareight is completely liquidated, United will be treated for tax purposes as if it sold the stock for an amount equal to the proceeds received. Assuming that the stock is a capital asset in United's hands and has been held for the required holding period, United will be taxed at the capital gains rate (see paragraph B.3). The schedule in Illustration 14 calculates this tax burden to United.

The final schedule in Illustration 15 calculates the NPP to United. After payment of the tax burden on the liquidation, United's NPP will be between $12,100,000 and $13,414,000.

7.202d *Presentation of Results*
Having completed the NPTC to General and the NPP to United, all that remains is to present the results in a format that is easy to understand. The graph in Illustration 16 hopefully conveys in a meaningful manner

Illustration 13
Calculation of Proceeds Available for Distribution *(In Thousands)*

Total selling price	$14,500	15,500	$16,500
Less: Total tax burden	(1,202)	(1,377)	(1,377)
Proceeds available for distribution	$13,298	$14,123	$15,123

Illustration 14
Calculation of United's Tax Burden Assuming Liquidation*
(In Thousands)

Total selling price	$14,500	$15,500	$16,500
Proceeds available for distribution	$13,298	$14,123	$15,123
Tax basis of stock	9,020	9,020	9,020
Taxable gain	4,278	5,103	6,103
Capital gains tax rate	28%	28%	28%
Tax burden on United	$ 1,198	$ 1,429	$ 1,709

*Exclusive of any burden associated with the minimum tax rules and the corporate tax preference cutback. See paragraph B. 9.

Illustration 15
Asset Acquisition—Calculation of NPP to United *(In Thousands)*

Selling price	$14,500	$15,500	$16,500
Liquidation proceeds	$13,298	$14,123	$15,123
Less: Tax burden	(1,198)	(1,429)	(1,709)
NPP	$12,100	$12,694	$13,414

Illustration 16

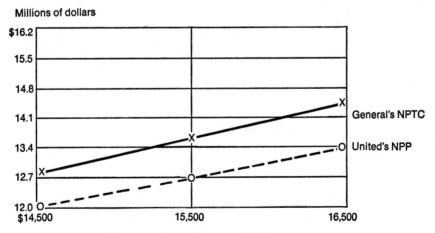

ASSET ACQUISITION

Net Present Tax Cost (NPTC) to General versus Net Present Proceeds (NPP) to United

Purchase price in thousands of dollars

the results. General's NPTC will be between $12,725,000 and $14,283,000 if an Asset Acquisition is consummated within the range of purchase prices analyzed. United's NPP (assuming liquidation) would be somewhere between $12,100,000 and $13,414,000.

7.203   338 Transaction

7.203a   Introduction
In order to comparatively analyze a stock deal (338 Transaction or a Stock Acquisition) versus an asset deal, General must assume that it will purchase the same assets and liabilities in both types of deals. Typically, a target has deferred taxes recorded on its books. However, this does not affect the comparability of the transactions. Why is this so? The deferred tax category is merely an accounting technique for recognizing timing differences between book and tax income with the most significant timing difference usually being accelerated depreciation. The cost analysis we are performing takes into account such differences.

7.203b   NPTC
General's first step in analyzing this type of deal was to compute the NPTC. The NPTC equals the present cash outflow associated with the acquisition less the present value of the future tax benefits that arise due to the fact that certain of the target's assets can be depreciated for tax purposes. The acquiring company in this type of acquisition will take a basis in the assets of the target company equal to the price paid for the stock adjusted for any liability associated with recapture by the target on the Section 338 deemed sale. The calculation of the adjusted purchase price is given in Illustration 17. Based on the adjusted purchase prices in Illustration 17, the buyer came up with preliminary allocations of the adjusted purchase price to the various asset categories (see Illustration 18). As discussed previously, it is reasonable to assume

Illustration 17
Calculation of Adjusted Purchase Price
(In Thousands)

Purchase price	$14,500	15,500	$16,500
Section 1245 recapture tax*	$ 1,175	1,350	1,350
Investment tax credits recaptured*	27	27	27
Adjusted purchase price	$15,702	$16,877	$17,877

*Calculated in paragraph 7.202c.

Illustration 18
Allocation of Adjusted Purchase Price to Asset Categories
(In Thousands)

Purchase price	$14,500	15,500	$16,500
Accounts receivable	$ 3,000	$ 3,000	$ 3,000
Inventory	6,750	6,750	6,750
Prepaid expenses	250	250	250
Accounts payable	(2,000)	(2,000)	(2,000)
Net working capital	8,000	8,000	8,000
Property, plant, and equipment:			
Land	250	250	250
Vehicles	100	100	100
Office equipment	100	100	100
Machinery and equipment	3,060	3,400	3,600
Buildings and improvements	3,890	4,350	4,600
Total	7,400	8,200	8,650
Goodwill	302	677	1,227
Adjusted purchase price	$15,702	$16,877	$17,877

that the fair market values of certain assets (e.g., buildings and improvements, machinery and equipment, and goodwill) would be higher given a higher purchase price. Why? If a buyer is willing to pay a higher price, this generally indicates that he has higher expectations of the profit potential to be generated by the business' assets. Given this higher profit expectancy, the underlying business assets have more value to him. One might argue that any increase in value over the bottom figures is all attributable to the company's goodwill, but this probably does not reflect reality. Remember, these are preliminary estimates. If hard information (appraisals) were available as to the fair market values of the assets, this information should be used. If the sum of the appraised values differs from the assumed purchase price, then (1) a second tier allocation must be performed to determine the tax basis of the various asset categories (see paragraph 3.203) and (2) an allocation of value must be performed to determine the book value of the various asset categories (see paragraph C.201).

General's NPTC includes its adjusted purchase price for the stock reduced by the present value of the tax savings associated with depreciating the buildings and improvements and the machinery and equipment. In computing the depreciation of the building and improvements and the machinery and equipment, the tax basis used will be the values in Illustration 18 (see Illustrations 19 and 20).

Illustration 19
Calculation of the Net Present Value of the Tax Savings from the Depreciation Deductions for Buildings and Improvements
(Dollar Figures in Thousands)

		$14,500	$15,500	$16,500
Total purchase price		$14,500	$15,500	$16,500
Fair market value of buildings and improvements		3,890	4,350	4,600
	Year			
ACRS depreciation percentages	1	9%	9%	9%
for 18-year class of property	2	9	9	9
	3	8	8	8
	4	7	7	7
	5	6	6	6
	6	6	6	6
	7	5	5	5
	8	5	5	5
	9	5	5	5
	10	5	5	5
Depreciation deductions	1	$ 350	$ 392	$ 414
	2	350	392	414
	3	311	348	368
	4	272	305	322
	5	233	261	276
	6	233	261	276
	7	195	218	230
	8	195	218	230
	9	195	218	230
	10	195	218	230
Tax savings at 50%	1	175	196	207
	2	175	196	207
	3	156	174	184
	4	136	152	161
	5	117	131	138
	6	117	131	138
	7	97	109	115
	8	97	109	115
	9	97	109	115
	10	97	109	115
10% present value factors	1	.9091	.9091	.9091
	2	.8264	.8264	.8264
	3	.7513	.7513	.7513
	4	.6830	.6830	.6830
	5	.6209	.6209	.6209
	6	.5645	.5645	.5645
	7	.5132	.5132	.5132
	8	.4665	.4665	.4665
	9	.4241	.4241	.4241
	10	.3855	.3855	.3855

Illustration 19 (*concluded*)

	Year	$14,500	$15,500	$16,500
Total purchase price		$14,500	$15,500	$16,500
Fair market value of buildings and improvements		3,890	4,350	4,600
Present value of tax savings	1	159	178	188
	2	145	162	171
	3	117	131	138
	4	93	104	110
	5	72	81	86
	6	66	74	78
	7	50	56	59
	8	45	51	54
	9	41	46	49
	10	37	42	44
		$ 826	$ 924	$ 977

Illustration 20
Calculation of the Net Present Value of the Tax Savings from the Depreciation Deductions for Machinery and Equipment *(Dollar Figures in Thousands)*

	Year	$14,500	$15,500	$16,500
Total purchase price		$14,500	$15,500	$16,500
Fair market value of machinery and equipment		3,060	3,400	3,600
ACRS depreciation percentages	1	15%	15%	15%
for 5-year class of property	2	22	22	22
	3	21	21	21
	4	21	21	21
	5	21	21	21
Depreciation deductions	1	$ 459	$ 510	$ 540
	2	673	748	792
	3	643	714	756
	4	643	714	756
	5	643	714	756
Tax savings at 50%	1	230	255	270
	2	337	374	396
	3	321	357	378
	4	321	357	378
	5	321	357	378
10% present value factors	1	.9091	.9091	.9091
	2	.8264	.8264	.8264
	3	.7513	.7513	.7513
	4	.6830	.6830	.6830
	5	.6209	.6209	.6209
Present value of tax savings	1	$ 209	$ 232	$ 245
	2	278	309	327
	3	241	268	284
	4	219	244	258
	5	199	222	235
		$ 1,147	$ 1,275	$ 1,350

Illustration 21
338 Transaction—Calculation of NPTC *(In Thousands)*

Purchase prices	$14,500	$15,500	$16,500
Less: Present value of tax savings from depreciation deductions for:			
Vehicles*	(41)	(41)	(41)
Office equipment*	(37)	(37)	(37)
Machinery and equipment	(1,147)	(1,275)	(1,350)
Buildings and improvements	(826)	(924)	(977)
Plus: Tax on Section 1245			
Depreciation recapture	1,175	1,350	1,350
ITC recapture	27	27	27
NPTC	$13,651	$14,600	$15,472

*Calculated in paragraph 7.202b.

General's NPTC will be increased by the tax associated with depreciation and investment tax credit recapture (see Illustration 21). This tax burden was calculated in paragraph 7.202c. General's NPTC will range between $13,651,000 and $15,472,000 assuming a 338 Transaction is effected at a price between $14.5 and $16.5 million.

7.203c NPP

Having computed the NPTC for the buyer, the next step is to calculate the seller's NPP. The shareholders are selling their stock in a 338 Transaction. General has estimated that United's tax basis in its stock is $9,020,000. Given that the current corporate capital gains tax rules result in a 28 percent effective rate, United's tax burden will be between $1,534,000 and $2,094,000 (see Illustration 22).

Illustration 22
Calculation of Tax Burden to United *(In Thousands)*

Selling Price	$14,500	$15,500	$16,500
Tax basis of stock	9,020	9,020	9,020
Taxable gain	5,480	6,480	7,480
Alternative calculation			
Capital gains tax rate	28%	28%	28%
Tax burden to United	$ 1,534	$ 1,814	$ 2,094

*Exclusive of any burden asociated with the minimum tax rules and the corporate tax preference cutback. See paragraph B. 9.

Illustration 23
338 Transaction—Calculation of NPP *(In Thousands)*

Selling prices	$14,500	$15,500	$16,500
Less: Tax burden	(1,534)	(1,814)	(2,094)
NPP	$12,966	$13,686	$14,406

Deducting the tax burden from the selling price, the stockholders will net between $12,966,000 and $14,406,000 in a 338 Transaction (see Illustration 23).

7.203d   Presentation of Results

The NPTC and NPP are displayed in the same format used for an Asset Acquisition. General's NPTC will be between $13,651,000 and $15,472,000, whereas United's NPP will range between $12,966,000 and $14,406,000 (see Illustration 24).

Illustration 24

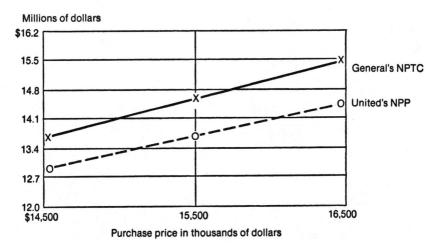

338 TRANSACTION

**Net Present Tax Cost (NPTC) to General versus
Net Present Proceeds (NPP) to United**

7.204 Stock Acquisition

7.204a NPTC

The NPTC in this type of acquisition is equal to the price paid for the stock less the present value of the tax savings from future depreciation deductions calculated using the target company's existing adjusted basis and depreciation methods. Since there is no disposition of assets by Mareight in this type of acquisition, there will be no depreciation or investment tax credit recapture.

Based on a review of Mareight's tax depreciation records, General calculates that the present value of the tax savings from future depreciation deductions will be as given in Illustration 25.

The NPTC for General can now be calculated (see Illustration 26). General's NPTC will range between $14,165,000 and $16,165,000 assuming a Stock Acquisition is consummated.

Illustration 25
Calculation of Present Value of Tax Savings For Depreciable Assets
(Dollar Figures in Thousands)

	Depreciation Deductions				10 Percent	Present
	Machinery and Equipment	Buildings and Improvements	Total	Tax Savings at 50 Percent	Present Value Factor	Value of Tax Savings
Year 1	$ 86	$ 71	$157	$78	.9091	$ 71
Year 2	86	71	157	78	.8264	64
Year 3	86	71	157	78	.7513	59
year 4	43	71	114	57	.6830	39
Year 5	43	71	114	57	.6209	35
Year 6	43	37	80	40	.5645	23
Year 7	43	37	80	40	.5132	21
Year 8		37	37	18	.4665	8
Year 9		37	37	18	.4241	8
Year 10		37	37	18	.3855	7
	$430	$540	$970			$335

Illustration 26
Stock Acquisition—Calculation of NPTC *(In Thousands)*

Purchase price	$14,500	$15,500	$16,500
Less: Present value of tax savings	(335)	(335)	(335)
NPTC	$14,165	$15,165	$16,165

7.204b NPP

The NPP to United in this type of acquisition are the same as under a 338 Transaction. The calculations are repeated in Illustrations 27 and 28. United's NPP will fall between $12,966,000 and $14,406,000 in a Stock Acquisition.

Illustration 27
Calculation of Tax Burden to United* *(In Thousands)*

Selling price	$14,500	$15,500	$16,500
Tax basis of stock	9,020	9,020	9,020
Taxable gain	5,480	6,480	7,480
Alternative calculation			
Capital gains tax rate	28%	28%	28%
Tax burden to United	$ 1,534	$ 1,814	$ 2,094

*Exclusive of any burden associated with the minimum tax rules and the corporate tax preference cutback. See paragraph B. 9.

Illustration 28
Stock Acquisition—Calculation of NPP *(In Thousands)*

Selling price	$14,500	$15,500	$16,500
Less: Tax burden	(1,534)	(1,814)	(2,094)
NPP	$12,966	$13,686	$14,406

7.204c Presentation of Results

The results of the NPTC and NPP analysis are displayed in Illustration 29.

Illustration 29

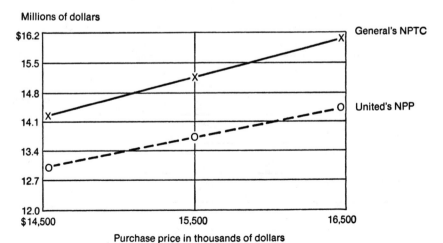

STOCK ACQUISITION

**Net Present Tax Cost (NPTC) to General versus
Net Present Proceeds (NPP) to United**

7.205   Comparative Analysis

The results of the cost analysis are displayed in the graphs shown in Illustrations 30 and 31. The NPTC comparative analysis graph shows a number of things to the decision maker. First it indicates that, all other considerations aside, it is in General's best interest to negotiate the deal as an Asset Acquisition. Second, it permits the decision maker to easily compare costs assuming different purchase prices and acquisition methods. For example, the NPTC for an Asset Acquisition assuming a $16.5 million purchase price is $14.3 million. If General buys Mareight's stock and makes a 338 election, the NPTC will be greater than $14.3 million unless the purchase price is less than approximately $15.4 million. Third, the NPTC comparative analysis indicates clearly that the acquiring company should lean towards a 338 Transaction rather than a Stock Acquisition. The NPP comparative analysis also reveals a number of facts. It indicates that United will prefer a Stock Acquisition or a 338 Transaction under any purchase price being considered, all other things being equal. Furthermore, the NPP comparative analysis graph allows the decision maker to understand the trade-offs that the target's shareholders are facing. The NPP in a Stock Acquisition or a 338 Transaction clearly exceed the NPP in an Asset Acqkuisition in all cases. How much is a Stock Acquisition or 338 Transaction worth to United? It is apparent from the graph that a Stock Acquisition or 338

Illustration 30

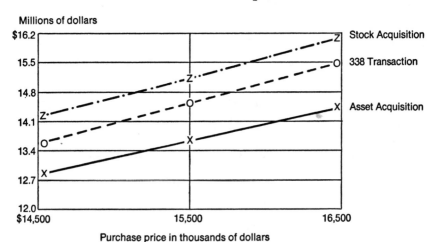

COMPARATIVE ANALYSIS

**Net Present Tax Cost (NPTC) to General
Under the Three Alternate Acquisition Methods**

Illustration 31

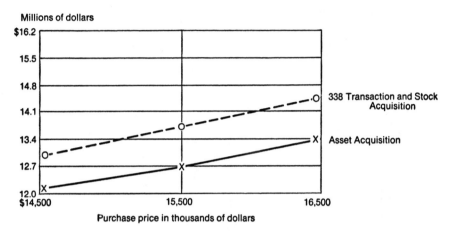

COMPARATIVE ANALYSIS

**Net Present Proceeds (NPP) to United
Under the Three Alternate Acquisition Methods**

Transaction at any price generates NPPs that approximate the NPPs from an Asset Acquisition completed at a purchase price approximately $1,400,000 greater. Finally, the NPP comparative analysis shows that United will be indifferent as to General's election to treat a stock acquisition as an asset purchase under Section 338.

7.3   THE ACQUISITION MODEL

Having completed the cost analysis and chosen the range of likely purchase prices, General developed the acquisition model for Mareight Corporation. Ordinarily, General would run the model for each of the three acquisition methods. However, for illustrative purposes we will assume that after reviewing the cost analysis, General's management decided to negotiate only on the basis that the acquisition would be effected as a straightforward Asset Acquisition. Therefore, the analysis that follows will focus solely on that method.

In developing the model, General devised Best Case, Most Likely Case, and Worst Case operating scenarios (see paragraph 7.303). These scenarios were computed two ways for a given purchase price: (1) excluding any cost savings associated with the acquisition and (2) including all cost savings associated with the acquisition.

Illustration 32
Internal Rates of Return Available on Proposed Acquisition of Mareight Corporation in an Asset Acquisition

	Purchase Price in Thousands		
	$14,500	$15,500	$16,500
Including cost savings:			
Best Case			
Most Likely Case			
Worst Case			
Excluding cost savings:			
Best Case			
Most Likely Case			
Worst Case			

7.301   Critical Information Sought

The end product that management desired in reviewing this acquisition was a matrix of rates of return available to General given different operating scenarios and purchase prices for the acquisition method considered. This matrix (see Illustration 32) would ultimately be converted to a graph that would vividly display the trade-offs between returns available and the purchase price.

7.302   Minimum Return Sought

At the time General began investigating the acquisition, its treasurer's department estimated the company's weighted-average cost of capital to be approximately 14.0 percent. Most members of top management felt that this should be the cutoff return sought by the company. This determination was based on their subjective evaluation that the risk associated with Mareight's business was approximately the same as that of General's existing businesses.

7.303   Development of Operating Scenarios

In this case General's management decided that there was only one variable that they felt should be modified to present Best, Worst, and Most Likely Cases. This variable was the rate of decline in unit sales. Management decided to prepare the three scenarios based on the following assumptions about the rate of decline:

	Rate of Decline
Best Case	.0%
Most Likely	1.5
Worst Case	3.0

All scenarios were developed in the same manner. Therefore, it is only necessary to review the procedure used to develop one scenario for one price (the Most Likely scenario for the $15.5 million purchase price).

7.304 Model Schedules

7.304a ITC and the Tax Basis of Certain Assets

This schedule computes the investment tax credits on Section 38 property and the tax basis of those assets for depreciation purposes (see Illustration 33).

The qualified investment in new Section 38 property is equal to the sum of (*a*) 100 percent of the basis of 10-year and 5-year recovery property and (*b*) 60 percent of the basis of 3-year recovery property. We will assume that all automobiles included in the vehicle category are used 100 percent for business purposes and that each cost less than $17,000. The qualified investment in used Section 38 property is limited to a maximum of $125,000 (see paragraph B.504).

In an Asset Acquisition a buyer is purchasing used Section 38 assets. Therefore, the maximum investment tax credit that the purchaser could receive is $12,500. However, General intends to elect to reduce the ITC taken by 2 percent for the used assets purchased and all new purchases of office equipment and machinery and equipment in years 1–10. Therefore, the ITC taken in Year 0 is only $10,000. General will reduce the tax basis of all new vehicles purchased in years 1–10 by one half the amount of ITC taken (see paragraphs B.401b and B.507).

One final point concerning the investment tax credit. The credit is not taken on replacement expenditures for buildings and improvements because these expenditures are not for qualified Section 38 property. Note also that the tax basis of property acquired in the acquisition and during the first year are combined for purposes of computing depreciation.

7.304b Depreciation Schedule

Having allocated the $15.5 million purchase price to the various asset categories and recomputed the tax basis of certain assets, depreciation and amortization expense must be calculated over the horizon of the analysis. Management determined that a 10-year period was the proper time period over which to calculate cash flows. Performing the depreciation calculations over this time span was complicated by the fact that General must provide capital to replace worn-out equipment and depreciate these new assets placed in service. The applicable depreciation

Illustration 33
ITC and the Tax Basis of Certain Assets (Dollar Figures in Thousands)

Three-Year Property	Year 0	Year 1	Year 2	Year 3	Year 4	Year 5	Year 6	Year 7	Year 8	Year 9	Year 10
Vehicles investment tax credit:											
Vehicles	$ 100	$ 0	$ 0	$ 0	$125	$ 0	$ 0	$ 0	$150	$ 0	$ 0
Percent qualifying for ITC	0%	60%	60%	60%	60%	60%	60%	60%	60%	60%	60%
Qualifying expenditure	0	0	0	0	75	0	0	0	90	0	0
ITC %	10%	10%	10%	10%	10%	10%	10%	10%	10%	10%	10%
ITC—vehicles	$ 0	$ 0	$ 0	$ 0	$ 7	$ 0	$ 0	$ 0	$ 9	$ 0	$ 0
Vehicles tax basis:											
Vehicles cost		$ 100	$ 0	$ 0	$125	$ 0	$ 0	$ 0	$150	$ 0	$ 0
Less: ITC × 50%		0	0	0	3	0	0	0	4	0	0
Vehicle tax basis		$ 100	$ 0	$ 0	$122	$ 0	$ 0	$ 0	$146	$ 0	$ 0
Five-year property											
Office equipment ITC:											
Office equipment	$ 100	$ 0	$ 0	$ 25	$ 0	$ 0	$ 35	$ 0	$ 0	$ 45	$ 0
Percent qualifying for ITC	0%	100%	100%	100%	100%	100%	100%	100%	100%	100%	100%

Qualifying expenditure	0	0	25	0	0	35	0	0	45	0
ITC %	8%	8%	8%	8%	8%	8%	8%	8%	8%	8%
ITC—office equipment	$ 0	$ 0	$ 2	$ 0	$ 0	$ 2	$ 0	$ 0	$ 3	$ 0
Office equipment tax basis	$ 100	$ 0	$ 25	$ 0	$ 0	$ 35	$ 0	$ 0	$ 45	$ 0
Machinery and equipment ITC										
Machinery and equipment	$3,000	$191	$202	$214	$227	$241	$255	$271	$287	$304
Percent qualifying for ITC	4%	100%	100%	100%	100%	100%	100%	100%	100%	100%
Qualifying expenditure	125	191	202	214	227	241	255	271	287	304
ITC %	8%	8%	8%	8%	8%	8%	8%	8%	8%	8%
ITC—machinery and equipment	$ 10	$ 15	$ 16	$ 17	$ 18	$ 19	$ 20	$ 21	$ 22	$ 24
Machinery and equipment tax basis	$3,180	$191	$202	$214	$227	$241	$255	$271	$287	$304
Investment Tax Credit Summary										
Vehicles	$ 0	$ 0	$ 0	$ 7	$ 0	$ 0	$ 0	$ 9	$ 0	$ 0
Office equipment	0	0	2	0	0	2	0	0	3	0
Machinery and equipment	24	15	16	17	18	19	20	21	22	24
Total investment tax credits	$ 24	$ 15	$ 18	$ 24	$ 18	$ 21	$ 20	$ 30	$ 25	$ 24

percentages used for the various asset categories are given in Illustration 34. For financial reporting purposes General would depreciate assets on a straight-line basis using the book depreciation percentages. For tax purposes, assets would be depreciated using the ACRS percentages listed in paragraph B.401b.

Let us review how the book and tax depreciation deductions are calculated for one asset category (machinery and equipment). If we turn back to paragraph 7.202a, we can see that machinery and equipment was valued at $3 million assuming a $15.5 million purchase price. Furthermore, paragraph 7.304a indicates that we expect to have expenditures for machinery and equipment of $180,000 in Year 1 and that for tax depreciation purposes the depreciable tax basis of machinery and equipment in Year 1 is $3,180,000 (original cost of machinery and equipment purchased [$3,000,000] plus the cost of additional machinery and equipment purchased in Year 1 [$180,000]). If we look at the schedule "Book and Tax Depreciation Deductions for Assets Placed in Service," we can see the depreciable tax basis and book value figures in Year 1 (see Illustration 35). Depreciation deductions for years 1 through 10 are then calculated based on the above applicable depreciation percentages. Depreciation deductions for expenditures for machinery and equipment in years 2 through 10 are calculated in a similar manner. The total column adds depreciation deductions for all years, and this total is carried up to the Summary of Book and Tax Depreciation and Amortization of Goodwill schedule (see Illustration 36). The Summary of Book and Tax Depreciation and Amortization of Goodwill schedule also calculates the amortization of goodwill each year for financial reporting purposes.

Illustration 34
Applicable Depreciation Percentages

Year	Vehicles		Office Equipment		Machinery and Equipment		Buildings and Improvements	
	ACRS	*Book*	*ACRS*	*Book*	*ACRS*	*Book*	*ACRS*	*Book*
1	25%	33%	15%	10%	15%	7%	9%	5%
2	38	33	22	10	22	7	9	5
3	37	33	21	10	21	7	8	5
4			21	10	21	7	7	5
5			21	10	21	7	6	5
6				10		7	6	5
7				10		7	5	5
8				10		7	5	5
9				10		7	5	5
10				10		7	5	5

Illustration 35
Book and Tax Depreciation Deductions for Assets Placed in Service *(Dollar Figures in Thousands)*

	Year 1	Year 2	Year 3	Year 4	Year 5	Year 6	Year 7	Year 8	Year 9	Year 10	Totals
Vehicles depreciable tax basis	$100	$0	$0	$122	$0	$0	$0	$146	$0	$0	$368
Depreciation year											
1	25	0	0								25
2	38	0	0								38
3	37	0	0								37
4			0	31	0	0					30
5			0	46	0	0					46
6			0	45	0	0					45
7			0	0	0	0	0				0
8			0	0	0	0	0	37	0		36
9			0	0	0	0	0	55	0	0	55
10			0	0	0	0	0	54	0	0	54
Vehicles book value	100	0	0	125	0	0	0	150	0	0	375
Book life in years	3										
Depreciation year											
1	33	0	0								33
2	33	0	0								33
3	33	0	0								33
4			0	41	0	0					41
5			0	41	0	0					41
6			0	41	0	0					41
7			0	0	0	0	0				0
8			0	0	0	0	0	50	0		49
9			0	0	0	0	0	50	0	0	49
10			0	0	0	0	0	50	0	0	49

Illustration 35 (concluded)

	Year 1	Year 2	Year 3	Year 4	Year 5	Year 6	Year 7	Year 8	Year 9	Year 10	Totals
Office equipment											
Depreciable tax basis	$100	0	$25	0	0	$35	0	0	$45	$0	$205
Depreciation year											
1	15										15
2	22	0									22
3	21	0	4								24
4	21	0	6	0							26
5	21	0	5	0	0						26
6	0	0	5	0	0	5					10
7	0	0	5	0	0	8	0				12
8	0	0	0	0	0	7	0	0			7
9	0	0	0	0	0	7	0	0	7	0	14
10	0	0	0	0	0	7	0	0	10	0	17
Office equipment book value	100	0	25	0	0	35	0	0	45	0	205
Book life in years	10										
Depreciation year											
1	10										10
2	10	0									10
3	10	0	3								12
4	10	0	3	0							12
5	10	0	3	0	0						12
6	10	0	3	0	0	4					16
7	10	0	3	0	0	4	0				16
8	10	0	3	0	0	4	0	0			16
9	10	0	3	0	0	4	0	0	5		20
10	10	0	3	0	0	4	0	0	5	0	20
Machinery and equipment:											
Depreciable tax basis	3,180	191	202	214	227	241	255	271	287	304	5,372
Depreciation year											
1	477										477
2	700	29									728
3	668	42	30								740
4	668	40	44	32							784
5	668	40	42	47	34						831
6	0	40	42	45	50	36					213
7	0	0	42	45	48	53	38				226
8	0	0	0	45	48	51	56	41			239
9	0	0	0	0	48	51	54	60	43		254
10	0	0	0	0	0	51	54	57	63	46	269

Machinery and equipment:	3,180	191	202	214	227	241	255	271	287	304	5,372
Book value	3,180										5,372
Book life in years	10										
Depreciation year											
1	212										212
2	212	13									224
3	212	13	13								238
4	212	13	13	14							252
5	212	13	13	14	15						267
6	212	13	13	14	15	16					283
7	212	13	13	14	15	16	17				300
8	212	13	13	14	15	16	17	18			318
9	212	13	13	14	15	16	17	18	19		337
10	212	13	13	14	15	16	17	18	19	20	358

Building and improvements:	3,820	21	22	24	25	27	28	30	32	34	4,063
Depreciable tax basis	3,820	21	22	24	25	27	28	30	32	34	4,063
Depreciation year											
1	344										343
2	344	2									345
3	306	2	2								309
4	267	2	2	2							273
5	229	2	2	2	2						236
6	229	1	2	2	2	2					238
7	191	1	1	2	2	2	3				202
8	191	1	1	1	2	2	3	3			203
9	191	1	1	1	1	2	2	3	3		205
10	191	1	1	1	1	2	2	2	3	3	207

Buildings and improvements:	3,820	21	22	24	25	27	28	30	32	34	4,063
Book value	3,820										4,063
Book life in years	10										
Depreciation year											
1	191										191
2	191	1									192
3	191	1	1								193
4	191	1	1	1							194
5	191	1	1	1	1						195
6	191	1	1	1	1	1					196
7	191	1	1	1	1	1	1				198
8	191	1	1	1	1	1	1	2			199
9	191	1	1	1	1	1	1	2	2		201
10	191	1	1	1	1	1	1	2	2	2	203

Illustration 36
Summary of Book and Tax Depreciation and Amortization of Goodwill (In Thousands)

		Year 0	Year 1	Year 2	Year 3	Year 4	Year 5	Year 6	Year 7	Year 8	Year 9	Year 10
Land		$ 250										
Vehicles		100										
Office equipment		100			$ 25	$ 125		$ 35		$150	$ 45	
Machinery and equipment		3,000	$180	$ 191	202	214	$ 227	241	$255	271	287	$304
Buildings and improvements		3,800	20	21	22	24	25	27	28	30	32	34
Goodwill		250										
Capital expenditures		$7,500	$200	$ 212	$ 249	$ 363	$ 252	$303	$283	$451	$364	$338
Calculation of Book Depreciation												
Vehicles	3 years		$ 33	$ 33	$ 33	$ 41	$ 41	$ 41	$ 16	$ 49	$ 49	$ 49
Office equipment	10 years		10	10	12	12	12	16		16	20	20
Machinery and equipment	15 years		212	224	238	252	267	283	300	318	337	358
Buildings and improvements	20 years		191	192	193	194	195	196	198	199	201	203
Total book depreciation			$446	$ 459	$ 476	$ 499	$ 515	$536	$514	$582	$607	$630
Calculation of Tax Depreciation												
Vehicles	3 years		$ 25	$ 38	$ 37	$ 30	$ 46	$ 45	$ 12	$ 36	$ 55	$ 54
Office equipment	5 years		15	22	24	26	26	10		7	14	17
Machinery and equipment	5 years		477	728	740	784	831	213	226	239	254	269
Buildings and improvements	18 years		343	345	309	273	236	238	202	203	205	207
Total tax depreciation			$860	$1,133	$1,110	$1,113	$1,139	$506	$440	$485	$528	$547
Calculation of Amortization of Goodwill												
Goodwill		$ 250										
Amortization period in years		40										
Annual amortization			$ 6	$ 6	$ 6	$ 6	$ 6	$ 6	$ 6	$ 6	$ 6	$ 6
Total book depreciation and amortization			$452	$ 465	$ 482	$ 505	$ 521	$542	$520	$588	$613	$636

7.304c   *Tax Benefit of Accelerated Depreciation*

The difference between book and tax depreciation results in considerable savings in taxes during the years immediately following the acquisition. The benefit is equal to the difference between tax and book depreciation multiplied by the marginal tax rate (see paragraph 6.606). In this case the marginal tax rate will be assumed to be 50 percent (46 percent federal tax rate plus an 8 percent state and local tax rate that is tax effected for federal tax purposes). Many companies in performing cash flow analyses on projects will use their "effective tax rate" in making calculations such as these. This is not proper because the effective tax rate is really an average tax rate for the company. The marginal tax rate is the correct rate to use. Items that effectively lower a company's tax rate should be treated separately in any analysis (e.g., investment tax credit). Note that the tax benefit of accelerated depreciation reverses in six years on an absolute basis for the whole company. However, the benefit does not reverse for buildings and improvements anytime over the 10-year period (see Illustration 37).

7.304d   *Tax Burden of Goodwill*

This schedule calculates the tax burden associated with goodwill (see paragraph 3.403c) based on the amortization figures generated in the Depreciation Schedule. Goodwill is an item that must be amortized for financial reporting purposes but is not a deductible expense for tax purposes. Thus, an amortization number is computed only for book purposes. Since goodwill cannot be deducted for tax purposes, there is a tax burden associated with goodwill (see paragraph 6.606). This burden is equal to the yearly book amortization figure multiplied by the marginal tax rate (see Illustration 38).

7.304e   *Forecast Income Statements*

The major assumptions used in preparing this schedule include the following:

a. Mareight's Most Likely Case scenario for unit volumes is forecasted to be a decline of 1.5 percent compounded annually. (All volumes are rounded down to the nearest million.)

b. Unit prices are assumed to rise at the 6 percent forecasted inflation rate.

c. Freight and returns have historically averaged 3.1 percent and 1.1 percent of total gross sales. These percentages are forecast to remain unchanged.

d. Over the last three years Mareight's gross margin percentage has fluctuated between 29.4 percent and 28.9 percent. General's

Illustration 37
Tax Benefit of Accelerated Depreciation (Dollar Figures in Thousands)

	Year 1	Year 2	Year 3	Year 4	Year 5	Year 6	Year 7	Year 8	Year 9	Year 10
Tax depreciation	$860	$1,133	$1,110	$1,113	$1,139	$506	$440	$485	$528	$547
Book depreciation	446	459	476	499	515	536	514	582	607	630
Difference	414	674	634	614	624	(30)	(74)	(97)	(79)	(83)
Times 50% tax rate	50%	50%	50%	50%	50%	50%	50%	50%	50%	50%
Tax benefit of accelerated depreciation	$207	$ 337	$ 317	$ 307	$ 312	$ (15)	$ (37)	$ (49)	$ (40)	$ (42)

Illustration 38
Tax Burden of Goodwill (Dollar Figures in Thousands)

	Year 1	Year 2	Year 3	Year 4	Year 5	Year 6	Year 7	Year 8	Year 9	Year 10
Amortization of goodwill	$ 6	$ 6	$ 6	$ 6	$ 6	$ 6	$ 6	$ 6	$ 6	$ 6
Tax rate	50%	50%	50%	50%	50%	50%	50%	50%	50%	50%
Tax burden of goodwill	$ 3	$ 3	$ 3	$ 3	$ 3	$ 3	$ 3	$ 3	$ 3	$ 3

management believes that the 29.4 percent is the better figure to use for forecasting purposes. Mareight uses FIFO accounting.

e. The depreciation and amortization figures appearing on the income statement represent book depreciation and amortization calculated in a prior schedule.

f. Selling, general, and administrative expenses are assumed to increase at a 6 percent compound annual rate.

The net result of our assumptions is that operating profit increases from $3,192 in Year 1 to $3,351 in Year 10 reflecting a compound annual growth rate of only .5 percent. This rate of growth lags the inflation rate of 6 percent primarily because of the projected decline in volume. General's management believes that Mareight will not be able to increase prices on their products fast enough to maintain the current operating profit to net sales ratio of 11.8 percent. Industry overcapacity will prevent gross margins from increasing to cover rising selling, general, and administrative expenses (see Illustration 39).

7.304f   Current Tax Liability

In order to calculate the current tax liability, Mareight's operating profit must be multiplied by the company's marginal tax rate (50 percent) adjusted for the tax effects of permanent and timing differences between pretax accounting income and taxable income (see paragraph 6.606) and reduced by the amount of tax credits available. We did not take into account any tax burden associated with the minimum tax rules or the corporate tax preference cutback (see paragraph B.9). The tax effects of both goodwill and accelerated depreciation were calculated on the Tax Burden of Goodwill Schedule and the Tax Benefit of Accelerated Depreciation schedules.

The current year's tax liability is not equal to the tax provision which would be calculated under generally accepted accounting principles. Furthermore, the average income tax liability is also not a figure that would be computed under generally accepted accounting principles. In the Mareight case a simple assumption is made that a year's average income tax liability is equal to 50 percent of the current income tax liability. The reason for generating this figure is to determine how much short-term financing the government is providing over the course of a year (see Illustration 40).

7.304g   Forecast Average Working Capital

The Forecast Average Working Capital schedule is designed to calculate changes in Mareight's working capital requirements by estimating each

Illustration 39
Forecast Income Statements (Dollar Figures in Thousands)

	Year 1	Year 2	Year 3	Year 4	Year 5	Year 6	Year 7	Year 8	Year 9	Year 10
Unit volume in millions:										
Product A	202	198	195	192	189	186	183	180	177	174
Product B	102	100	98	96	94	92	90	88	86	84
Total	304	298	293	288	283	278	273	268	263	258
Unit prices (in cents):										
Product A	7.10	7.53	7.98	8.46	8.97	9.51	10.08	10.68	11.32	12.00
Product B	14.40	15.26	16.18	17.15	18.18	19.27	20.43	21.66	22.96	24.34
Gross Sales:										
Product A	$14,342	$14,909	$15,561	$16,243	$16,953	$17,688	$18,446	$19,224	$20,036	$20,880
Product B	14,688	15,260	15,856	16,464	17,089	17,728	18,387	19,060	19,745	20,445
Total	29,030	30,169	31,417	32,707	34,042	35,416	36,833	38,284	39,781	41,325
Less:										
Freight	898	934	972	1,012	1,054	1,096	1,140	1,185	1,231	1,279
Returns	318	331	345	359	374	389	404	420	437	454
Net sales	27,814	28,904	30,100	31,336	32,614	33,931	35,289	36,679	38,113	39,592
Cost of goods sold	19,636	20,406	21,250	22,123	23,025	23,955	24,914	25,895	26,907	27,951
Gross profit	8,178	8,498	8,850	9,213	9,589	9,976	10,375	10,784	11,206	11,641
Depreciation and amortization	452	465	482	505	521	542	520	588	613	636
Selling, General and Administrative expenses	4,534	4,806	5,094	5,399	5,722	6,065	6,428	6,813	7,221	7,654
Operating profit	$ 3,192	$ 3,227	$ 3,274	$ 3,309	$ 3,346	$ 3,369	$ 3,427	$ 3,383	$ 3,372	$ 3,351
Gross profit %	29.4%	29.4%	29.4%	29.4%	29.4%	29.4%	29.4%	29.4%	29.4%	29.4%

Illustration 40
Current Tax Liability *(Dollar Figures in Thousands)*

	Year 1	Year 2	Year 3	Year 4	Year 5	Year 6	Year 7	Year 8	Year 9	Year 10
Operating profit	$3,192	$3,227	$3,274	$3,309	$3,346	$3,369	$3,427	$3,383	$3,372	$3,351
Tax rate	50%	50%	50%	50%	50%	50%	50%	50%	50%	50%
Taxes at normal rate	1,596	1,613	1,637	1,654	1,673	1,684	1,713	1,691	1,686	1,675
Less: Investment tax credit	24	15	18	24	18	21	20	30	25	24
Plus: Permanent difference Tax burden of goodwill	3	3	3	3	3	3	3	3	3	3
Adjusted tax provision	1,575	1,601	1,622	1,633	1,658	1,666	1,696	1,664	1,664	1,654
Less: Timing difference Tax benefit of accelerated depreciation	207	337	317	307	312	(15)	(37)	(49)	(40)	(42)
Current year's tax liability	$1,368	$1,264	$1,305	$1,326	$1,346	$1,681	$1,733	$1,713	$1,704	$1,696
Average income tax liability	$ 684	$ 632	$ 652	$ 663	$ 673	$ 840	$ 866	$ 856	$ 852	$ 848

working capital component: accounts receivable, inventory, prepaid expenses, accounts payable and accrued expenses, and income taxes payable (see Illustration 41).

Mareight's receivables have averaged 42 days sales outstanding over the last three years and are not anticipated to change. Therefore, Mareight's average receivables are estimated by multiplying net sales times 42 days/365 days.

Mareight's average inventory investment is thought to be a function of cost of goods sold and the number of times inventory turns over. Mareight's inventory has turned an average of 3.0 times over the last three years. Given this assumption, the average inventory figure is calculated by dividing cost of goods sold by the number of turns.

Mareight's prepaid expense figure jumped from $227 in 1983 to $396 in 1984. General believes that this figure is an anomaly and that in the future prepaid expenses will return to an average 1.0 percent of total costs excluding depreciation.

Accounts payable and accrued expenses are a function of costs and the length of time Mareight takes to pay bills. Mareight generally pays for items that are included in cost of goods sold in 30 days on average (12 payments a year). However, Mareight pays for costs included in selling, general, and administrative expenses in 20 days on average (18 payments a year) because of the fact that salaries are such a large part of these costs. Mareight's formula for computing the average level of accounts payable and accrued expenses is:

(Cost of goods sold/12) + (Selling, general, and administrative expenses/18)

7.304b Operating Cash Flow Forecast

Generally, this schedule summarizes the data from the prior schedules. However, two key items affecting the returns available for the acquisition are treated for the first time on this schedule: (1) the residual value of the business at the end of the time horizon of the analysis and (2) the cash flows resulting from operating synergies connected with the acquisition.

General's management tends to be conservative in making projections. Therefore, they have opted to assume that Mareight will be worth an amount equal to its depreciated book value at the end of 10 years. They have elected to ignore the tax effects associated with selling the company at that price because of the nature of such a guesstimate. Furthermore, they do not presently intend to sell the company at that time. This residual value has a working capital component and a fixed asset plus goodwill component. The working capital component is drawn from the Forecast Average Working Capital schedule while the

Illustration 41
Forecast Average Working Capital *(In Thousands)*

	Year 0	Year 1	Year 2	Year 3	Year 4	Year 5	Year 6	Year 7	Year 8	Year 9	Year 10
Gross sales		$29,030	$30,169	$31,417	$32,707	$34,042	$35,416	$36,833	$38,284	$39,781	$41,325
Cost of goods sold		19,636	20,406	21,250	22,123	23,025	23,955	24,914	25,895	26,907	27,951
Selling, general, and administrative expenses		4,534	4,806	5,094	5,399	5,722	6,065	6,428	6,813	7,221	7,654
Working capital:											
Receivables	$3,000	$ 3,340	$ 3,471	$ 3,615	$ 3,763	$ 3,917	$ 4,075	$ 4,238	$ 4,405	$ 4,577	$ 4,755
Inventory	6,750	6,545	6,802	7,083	7,374	7,675	7,985	8,304	8,631	8,969	9,317
Prepaid expenses	250	265	276	288	301	315	329	343	358	374	390
Accounts payable and accrued expenses	(2,000)	(1,888)	(1,967)	(2,053)	(2,143)	(2,236)	(2,333)	(2,433)	(2,536)	(2,643)	(2,754)
Average income tax liability		(684)	(632)	(652)	(663)	(673)	(840)	(866)	(856)	(852)	(848)
Average working capital	8,000	7,578	7,950	8,281	8,632	8,998	9,216	9,586	10,002	10,425	10,860
Prior year's average working capital		8,000	7,578	7,950	8,281	8,632	8,998	9,216	9,586	10,002	10,425
Increase (decrease) over prior year	$8,000	$ (422)	$ 372	$ 331	$ 351	$ 366	$ 218	$ 370	$ 416	$ 423	$ 435
Days sales outstanding	42	42	42	42	42	42	42	42	42	42	42
Inventory turns	3	3	3	3	3	3	3	3	3	3	3

other component is calculated by summing the purchase price and capital expenditures for fixed assets and goodwill over the 10 years and subtracting all applicable book depreciation and amortization (see Illustration 42).

Once the cash flows excluding synergies have been tabulated and an IRR calculated, the cash flows from cost savings that have been separately modeled can be added and a new IRR calculated. For General the cost savings are an important part of the transaction, raising the IRR from 12.1 percent to 17.0 percent for the Most Likely Case given a $15.5 million purchase price (see Illustrations 43 and 44).

7.304i   Company Cash Flow Forecast

The Company Cash Flow Forecast adds the cash flows associated with financing the acquisition to the Operating Cash Flow Forecast. Remember that the analysis in this case is performed two ways (1) excluding any cost savings and (2) including all cost savings. The Company Cash Flow Forecast is calculated in both cases. For purposes of illustration, the Company Cash Flow Forecast excluding any cost savings is presented in Illustration 45.

General anticipates financing the acquisition by having Mareight borrow $8 million payable over 10 years at 12 percent. Repayments will be made in four yearly payments of $2 million starting at the end of Year 7. These funds will be used to reduce General's investment in Mareight. The borrowings, return of capital, related interest, and repayments appear in the Company Cash Flow Forecast. Interest income is also calculated in this schedule based on the following formula:

[(Beginning cash balance + Ending cash balance)/2] × Interest rate

In calculating interest income, General assumed an interest rate of 10 percent. Once interest income and expense are added to the model, a new tax liability must be calculated. In an effort to make the Company Balance Sheets Forecast conform as closely as possible to generally accepted accounting principles (GAAP), the tax provision is calculated in accordance with GAAP and the tax benefit associated with accelerated depreciation is listed separately as "Deferred taxes." Mechanically, the tax provision is calculated by adding the "Adjusted tax provision" line from the Current Tax Liability schedule with the result of the following calculation:

Interest expense	+
Interest income	+ _____
Total	
Tax rate	_____ 50%
Tax effect	_____

Illustration 42
Operating Cash Flow Forecast (In Thousands)

	Year 0	Year 1	Year 2	Year 3	Year 4	Year 5	Year 6	Year 7	Year 8	Year 9	Year 10
Operating profit		$ 3,192	$ 3,227	$ 3,274	$ 3,309	$ 3,346	$ 3,369	$ 3,427	$3,383	$3,372	$ 3,351
Taxes at normal rate		1,596	1,613	1,637	1,654	1,673	1,684	1,713	1,691	1,686	1,675
Earnings after taxes		1,596	1,614	1,637	1,655	1,673	1,685	1,714	1,692	1,686	1,676
Depreciation and amortization		452	465	482	505	521	542	520	588	613	636
Investment tax credit		24	15	18	24	18	21	20	30	25	24
Tax benefit of accelerated depreciation		207	337	317	307	312	(15)	(37)	(49)	(40)	(42)
Residual value:											
Working capital											10,860
Net property, plant, equipment											5,191
Less:											
Tax burden of goodwill		3	3	3	3	3	3	3	3	3	3
Increase in working capital	8,000	(422)	372	331	351	366	218	370	416	423	435
Capital expenditures	7,500	200	212	249	363	252	303	283	451	364	338
Cash flow:	$(15,500)	$ 2,498	$ 1,844	$ 1,871	$ 1,774	$ 1,903	$ 1,709	$ 1,561	$ 1,391	$1,494	$17,569
Cumulative cash flow	$(15,500)	$(13,002)	$(11,158)	$(9,287)	$(7,513)	$(5,610)	$(3,901)	$(2,340)	$ (949)	$ 545	$18,114
Internal rate of return	12.1 %										

Illustration 43
Analysis of Cash Flows From Synergies (In Thousands)

Anticipated Savings	Year 1	Year 2	Year 3	Year 4	Year 5	Year 6	Year 7	Year 8	Year 9	Year 10
Sales force reduction	$ 0	$ 854	$ 905	$ 959	$1,017	$1,078	$1,143	$1,211	$1,284	$1,361
Duplicated administrative expenses	100	384	407	432	458	485	514	545	578	612
Packaging savings	100	212	225	238	252	268	284	301	319	338
Pretax savings	200	1,450	1,537	1,629	1,727	1,831	1,941	2,057	2,181	2,311
Tax on savings at 50% rate	100	725	768	814	863	915	970	1,028	1,090	1,155
Cash flow from synergies	$100	$ 725	$ 769	$ 815	$ 864	$ 916	$ 971	$1,029	$1,091	$1,156

Illustration 44
Calculation of Internal Rate of Return Including All Expected Cost Savings (In Thousands)

	Year 0	Year 1	Year 2	Year 3	Year 4	Year 5	Year 6	Year 7	Year 8	Year 9	Year 10
Cash flow before synergies	$(15,500)	$2,498	$1,844	$1,871	$1,774	$1,903	$1,709	$1,561	$1,391	$1,494	$17,569
Cash flow from synergies	0	100	725	769	815	864	916	971	1,029	1,091	1,156
Total cash flows	$(15,500)	$2,598	$2,569	$2,640	$2,589	$2,767	$2,625	$2,532	$2,420	$2,585	$18,725
Internal rate of return	17.0%										

Illustration 45
Company Cash Flow Forecast (In Thousands)

	Year 0	Year 1	Year 2	Year 3	Year 4	Year 5	Year 6	Year 7	Year 8	Year 9	Year 10
SOURCES OF FUNDS:											
Operating profit		$3,192	$3,227	$3,274	$3,309	$3,346	$3,369	$3,427	$3,383	$3,372	$3,351
Interest expense		(960)	(960)	(960)	(960)	(960)	(960)	(960)	(720)	(480)	(240)
Interest income		80	240	401	568	745	929	999	960	932	922
Pre-tax income		2,312	2,507	2,715	2,917	3,131	3,338	3,466	3,623	3,824	4,033
Tax provision		1,135	1,241	1,342	1,437	1,550	1,650	1,715	1,784	1,890	1,995
Net income		1,177	1,266	1,373	1,480	1,581	1,688	1,751	1,839	1,934	2,038
Proceeds from equity Funding	$8,000										
Proceeds from borrowing		446	459	476	499	515	536	514	582	607	630
Depreciation		6	6	6	6	6	6	6	6	6	6
Amortization											
Deferred taxes		207	337	317	307	312	(15)	(37)	(49)	(40)	(42)
Total sources	8,000	1,836	2,068	2,172	2,292	2,414	2,215	2,234	2,378	2,507	2,632
USES OF FUNDS:											
Repayment of debt		200	212	249	363	252	303	283	451	364	338
Capital expenditures								2,000	2,000	2,000	2,000
Increase (decrease) in working capital:											
Accounts receivable		340	131	144	148	154	158	163	167	172	178
Inventory		(205)	257	281	291	301	310	319	327	338	348
Prepaid expenses		15	11	12	13	14	14	14	15	16	16
Accounts payable and accrued expenses		112	(79)	(86)	(90)	(93)	(97)	(100)	(103)	(107)	(111)
Average income tax liability		(244)	(28)	(100)	(95)	(98)	(259)	(61)	(91)	(102)	(111)
Subtotal		18	292	251	267	278	126	335	315	317	320
Dividends											
Return of capital	8,000										
Total uses	8,000	218	504	500	630	530	429	2,618	2,766	2,681	2,658
Increase (decrease) in cash	0	1,618	1,564	1,672	1,662	1,884	1,786	(384)	(388)	(174)	(26)
Cash—beginning	0	0	1,618	3,182	4,854	6,516	8,400	10,186	9,802	9,414	9,240
Cash—ending	$0	$1,618	$3,182	$4,854	$6,516	$8,400	$10,186	$9,802	$9,414	$9,240	$9,214

However, for purposes of calculating the increase or decrease in working capital, the average income tax liability is calculated without excluding the tax benefit of accelerated depreciation. Moreover, the tax effect of the net interest income or expense is taken into account in arriving at the average income tax liability on this schedule.

7.304j   Company Balance Sheets Forecast

Based primarily on the Company Cash Flow Forecast, a Company Balance Sheets Forecast was prepared for Mareight. These balance sheets include General's intended financing for the acquisition. The Company Balance Sheets Forecast (excluding any cost savings of the acquisition) is presented in Illustration 46.

7.4   EVALUATING RISK

In an effort to help the decision makers understand the risk involved in the acquisition Best Case, Worst Case, and Most Likely Case scenarios were developed for Mareight. The only difference among the scenarios was the rate of decline in volume sales (see paragraph 7.303). No attempt was made to estimate a probability of any of the scenarios occurring. This probability estimation was left for the decision makers to subjectively determine.

General's management also had sensitivity analysis performed for a number of variables including residual value: selling, general, and administrative expenses: level of inventories: and so forth. However, for illustrative purposes only, the sensitivity analysis for changes in the gross margin from the Most Likely Case assumption are shown in Illustration 47 (assumes no cost savings). The matrix in Illustration 47 is converted to a graph in Illustration 48.

Illustration 47
Mareight Acquisition Internal Rates
of Return Assuming Percentage Increases
and Decreases from Most Likely
Case Gross Margin Assumption of 29.4 Percent

Gross Margin	Purchase Price		
Percentage	*$14,500*	*$15,500*	*$16,500*
+2	15.5%	14.5%	13.6%
+1	14.2	13.3	12.5
Most Likely Case	12.9	12.1	11.4
−1	11.7	10.9	10.3
−2	10.4	9.8	9.2

Illustration 46

Company Balance Sheets Forecast (In Thousands)

	Year 0	Year 1	Year 2	Year 3	Year 4	Year 5	Year 6	Year 7	Year 8	Year 9	Year 10
Assets											
Current assets:											
Cash and short-term investments	$ 0	$ 1,618	$ 3,182	$ 4,854	$ 6,516	$ 8,400	$10,186	$ 9,802	$ 9,414	$ 9,240	$ 9,214
Accounts receivable	3,000	3,340	3,471	3,615	3,763	3,917	4,075	4,238	4,405	4,577	4,755
Inventory	6,750	6,545	6,802	7,083	7,374	7,675	7,985	8,304	8,631	8,969	9,317
Prepaid expenses	250	265	276	288	301	315	329	343	358	374	390
Total current assets	10,000	11,768	13,731	15,840	17,954	20,307	22,575	22,687	22,808	23,160	23,676
Property, plant and equipment:											
Gross	7,250	7,450	7,662	7,911	8,274	8,526	8,829	9,112	9,563	9,927	10,265
Less: Accumulated depreciation	0	446	905	1,381	1,880	2,395	2,931	3,445	4,027	4,634	5,264
Net property, plant and equipment	7,250	7,004	6,757	6,530	6,394	6,131	5,898	5,667	5,536	5,293	5,001
Goodwill	250	244	238	232	226	220	214	208	202	196	190
Total assets	$17,500	$19,016	$20,726	$22,602	$24,574	$26,658	$28,687	$28,562	$28,546	$28,649	$28,867
Liabilities											
Current liabilities:											
Accounts payable and accrued expenses	$ 2,000	$ 1,888	$ 1,967	$ 2,053	$ 2,143	$ 2,236	$ 2,333	$ 2,433	$ 2,536	$ 2,643	$ 2,754
Income tax liability	0	244	272	372	467	565	824	885	976	1,078	1,189
Total current liabilities	2,000	2,132	2,239	2,425	2,610	2,801	3,157	3,318	3,512	3,721	3,943
Long-term debt	8,000	8,000	8,000	8,000	8,000	8,000	8,000	6,000	4,000	2,000	0
Deferred taxes	0	207	544	861	1,168	1,480	1,465	1,428	1,379	1,339	1,297
Total liabilities	10,000	10,339	10,783	11,286	11,778	12,281	12,622	10,746	8,891	7,060	5,240
Stockholder's Equity											
Capital stock	7,500	7,500	7,500	7,500	7,500	7,500	7,500	7,500	7,500	7,500	7,500
Retained earnings	0	1,177	2,443	3,816	5,296	6,877	8,565	10,316	12,155	14,089	16,127
Total equity	7,500	8,677	9,943	11,316	12,796	14,377	16,065	17,816	19,655	21,589	23,627
Total liabilities and stockholder's equity	$17,500	$19,016	$20,726	$22,602	$24,574	$26,658	$28,687	$28,562	$28,546	$28,649	$28,867

Illustration 48

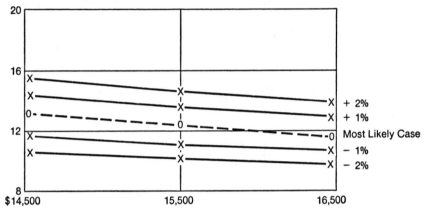

| SENSITIVITY ANALYSIS |

**Mareight Acquisition Internal Rates of Return Assuming
Percentage Increases and Decreases from Most
Likely Case Gross Margin Assumption of 29.4 Percent**

Internal rate of return (percent)

Purchase price in thousands of dollars

7.5 PRESENTING THE RESULTS

The final matrix for the acquisition assuming an Asset Acquisition appears in Illustration 49. This matrix is displayed in graphic form in Illustrations 50 and 51. The graphs in Illustrations 50 and 51 clearly display the trade-offs between returns available and purchase price given different operating scenarios. Theoretically, if there were no expected cost savings, General should not agree to purchase Mareight unless the purchase price is dropped to a point where the expected return for the most likely case equals the company's 14.0 percent required rate of return. In this case, that price (not shown on graph) would be approxi-

Illustration 49
Internal Rates of Return Available on Proposed
Acquisition of Mareight Corporation in an Asset Acquisition

	Purchase Price in Millions		
	$14.5	*$15.5*	*$16.5*
Including cost savings:			
Best Case	19.7%	18.6%	17.6%
Most Likely Case	18.0	17.0	16.0
Worst Case	16.7	15.7	14.8
Excluding cost savings:			
Best Case	14.9	14.1	13.3
Most Likely Case	12.9	12.1	11.4
Worst Case	11.2	10.5	9.8

Illustration 50

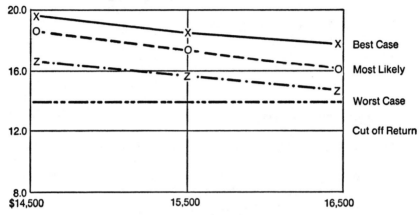

Mareight Acquisition Internal Rates of Return Including All Cost Savings

Illustration 51

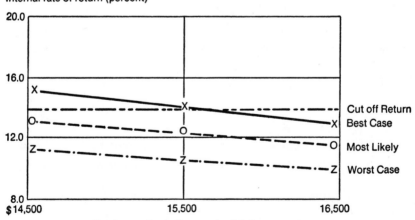

Mareight Acquisition Internal Rates of Return Excluding All Cost Savings

mately $13.25 million. However, United's management is demanding a premium price for Mareight because they understand that Mareight will become a more valuable property in General's hands. At a purchase price of $16.5 million, General calculates that under all three operating scenarios the expected return will surpass management's cutoff return of 14.0 percent. In theory, General's management would be correct in agreeing to pay United's asking price. In reality, General's management now has a good understanding of their position in looking to negotiate a final deal.

7.6   IMPACT ON GENERAL

Once the acquisition model has been completed and the risk analysis performed, the only remaining task is to analyze the effect of the transaction on General. The purpose of this analysis is to understand the transaction's impact on General's (1) earnings and/or earnings per share, (2) liquidity, and (3) overall financial strength (e.g., whether the acquisition will give rise to a change in the rating of the acquiring company's outstanding securities). The analysis is performed by consolidating Mareight's forecast balance sheets, income statements, and cash flow statements with General's forecast statements. This analysis is not shown here due to the limited impact that a $15–$16 million acquisition would have on General, a multibillion dollar company.

7.7   SUMMARY ANALYSIS

Having completed the financial analysis of Mareight, the decision makers at General can now make an informed decision about both the price to pay for Mareight and the method of effecting the transaction. Their informed judgment rests on the knowledge gained from answering the three basic questions.

1. What will the acquisition cost?
2. What return can we expect if we go ahead with the acquisition?
3. What is the probability of achieving the expected return?

The first question was answered through the cost analysis which produced a graph comparing the NPTC to General under the three alternate acquisition methods being considered (see paragraph 7.205). In addition, the cost analysis revealed how United would view the various transactions. The second and third questions were answered through the results produced from the acquisition model. The matrix of returns assuming various purchase prices and operating scenarios enabled management to understand the trade-offs that exist. The risk question was further addressed by performing sensitivity analysis on key operating variables.

Section Five

Conclusion

Chapter 8

Concluding Note

8.1 OTHER FACTORS TO CONSIDER

In addressing the pricing issue, many tax and accounting issues have been sidestepped that are very important such as: employee benefit plan liabilities, installment sales, contingent purchase prices, valuing inventories, and so on. However, the author believes that most acquisition technicians should be able to adapt the framework contained in this book to deal with such problems.

Since the book is financial in nature, there has been no discussion of the nonfinancial factors that affect the outcome of an acquisition. The purpose of this chapter is to provide some perspective for carrying out the financial analysis, make some observations on controversial acquisitions in the past, and discuss the current stock market's impact on pricing.

8.2 FINANCIAL ANALYSIS IN PERSPECTIVE

The financial analysis advocated in this book is of limited value unless the acquiring company frames the assumptions for the analysis only after a detailed review of management's operating philosophy, policies, practices, procedures, and controls. Evaluating target company management is probably the single most important exercise that an acquiring company has to perform before deciding on the acquisition, unless the target is a turnaround situation. Why? Financial forecasts do not make acquisitions work, people do! Let us take a look at some examples to understand the problem. First, two examples where the outcome of the acquisition is undetermined at this time.

- Rite Aid, a company with $1.3 billion in sales, was looking to acquire other operations early in 1984 because of a declining rate of growth in its basic drug store business. As a result it purchased ADAP (formerly American Discount Auto Parts, Inc.), an auto parts chain with sales of $33 million, for $28 million in cash. The two companies have entirely different corporate cultures. Rite Aid is a typical billion dollar company with an impressive corporate headquarters, detailed financial reporting requirements for subsidiaries, and a hierarchical organization reporting structure. Rite Aid's management, in all likelihood, anticipates that there will be some synergies in the acquisition due to the fact that Rite Aid has existing store planning, advertising, and site location functions. Furthermore, since some auto supplies may be sold in its drugstores, there may be purchasing efficiencies. ADAP, on the other hand, is run in an informal manner by an entrepreneurial leader who is used to making his own decisions. He has negotiated the deal under assurances that Rite Aid would not interfere with his operation. If Rite Aid and ADAP's management have not clearly defined to each other their post-acquisition roles and relationships clearly, the potential exists for serious problems. For example, if Rite Aid wants ADAP to grow much more rapidly than it has in the past so that the acquisition can have a more meaningful impact on Rite Aid's overall financial results, or if ADAP has a bad quarter or year and Rite Aid decides to step in, the relationship between Rite Aid's and ADAP's management might sour. The effect of such a deterioration in the relationship is incalculable.[1]
- In June 1984, General Motors (GM) agreed to acquire Electronic Data Systems Corp. (EDS), a data services concern for approximately $2.5 billion. GM was seeking an acquisition at the time because it was flush with cash and devoid of any further opportunities within its own industry that it was not presently pursuing. The price paid by GM represented close to 33 times the target's estimated 1984 earnings. Initial announcements by GM's management were that GM would operate EDS as an independent subsidiary with an unusual degree of autonomy. However, GM also announced that the two companies' communications systems and personnel would be merged. The questions concerning post-acquisition roles and relationships are the same as the Rite Aid/ADAP example even though the acquisition is 90 times larger.[2]

Now let us turn to an acquisition that has to date proven unsuccessful because the post-acquisition roles were not clearly defined before the deal was consummated.

- Westinghouse purchased Unimation, Inc., from Condec Corp. for $107 million in 1983 in order to participate in the substantial growth expected in the robot market. At the time of the acquisition, Unimation was the number one robot maker in the United States with an estimated 30 percent share of the market. In analyzing the acquisition, Westinghouse expected Unimation to participate heavily in large proven robot markets such as the automobile industry. However, Westinghouse did not adequately discuss these plans with Unimation's founder and president, Joseph Engelberger, even though Mr. Engelberger's expertise was considered a valuable part of the deal. Mr. Engelberger, on the other hand, expected Westinghouse to provide substantial funding for Unimation to explore entirely new applications for robots. As a result of these differences a fallout ensued after the deal was completed, and Mr. Engelberger left Unimation. In analyzing the acquisition, Westinghouse also expected to implement its decision-making processes and compensation plans. Unfortunately, Unimation's software specialists, which Mr. Engelberger believed to be vital to the company, perceived the implementation of such plans and processes to be to their detriment. After encountering serious problems with this group, Westinghouse agreed to let these specialists form their own company to provide services for Unimation. The financial results of the acquisition have thus far been unsatisfactory. Unimation has lost money since the acquisition, and the company only expects to break even in a few years.[3]

Hopefully, the examples indicate that post-acquisition roles and relationships have to be worked out in some detail prior to closing the deal. Otherwise, in all likelihood the financial forecasts will not be met.

8.3 OBSERVATIONS FROM THE DECADES MOST CONTROVERSIAL ACQUISITIONS

Based on a review of the amount of press given major acquisitions since 1974, the author arrived at a list of the top 25 most controversial deals. This list is:

Mobil Oil—Marcor
General Electric—Utah International
Atlantic Richfield—Anaconda
McDermott—Babcock & Wilcox

Phillip Morris—7 UP
Exxon—Reliance Electric
RCA—CIT Financial
United Technologies—Carrier
American Express—Shearson
Dart—Kraft
Baldwin United—MGIC
DuPont—Conoco
U.S. Steel—Marathon Oil
Kennecott—Carborundum
Xerox—Crum & Foster
Fluor—St. Joe
Coca Cola—Columbia Pictures
Allied—Bendix
Texaco—Getty Oil
Beatrice—Esmark
SoCal—Gulf
Occidental Petroleum—Cities Service
Mobil Oil—Superior
General Motors—Electronic Data Systems
Nabisco—Standard Brands

The author believes that acquisitions included in the list confirm the notion that successful unrelated diversification is difficult to achieve. General Electric's acquisition of Utah International and RCA's acquisition of CIT can be cited as examples where the acquiring company was not pleased with the performance of an unrelated acquisition. Both companies have divested their acquisitions. Furthermore, acquisitions of companies operating in related fields do not necessarily ensure success. Phillip Morris acquired 7up for $520 million in 1978 fresh on the heels of its marketing coup with Miller Lite beer. At the time Phillip Morris believed it could transfer its marketing skills to 7up and score another huge success. However, the acquisition has not been profitable for the past five years under Phillip Morris stewardship due to the tough competition in the soft drink industry. The reader will undoubtedly note some winning deals and other losers in the list. The key point that the readers should note is that there are a fair proportion of each.

8.4 CURRENT STOCK MARKET'S IMPACT ON PRICING

A key concept that has not been addressed until now is the effect that the current stock market situation should have on pricing. For example, if the marketplace is valuing a company in a certain industry at a very high price/earnings multiple or if an acquisition of a similar company has recently occurred, how does this effect what one should pay? It should be obvious that if the marketplace is valuing the target such that the buyer cannot achieve a return equal to the buyer's cutoff return (see paragraph 6.3), the buyer should not get caught up in an emotional struggle and pass on the opportunity. However, assuming the marketplace is valuing the target such that the buyer's analysis indicates that attractive returns are available, how much should the buyer pay for the acquisition? Theoretically, the buyer could pay an amount that would result in the cutoff return for the acquisition given the Most Likely operating scenario. Practically speaking, the marketplace valuation is another input that the decision maker will use in negotiating the deal. The decision maker will know going into negotiations that he has some room to increase the price over the market's valuation. However, like all other buyers, he will be looking to pay the least amount possible.

8.5   CONCLUSION

The author does not offer a magic formula for pricing acquisitions because no such magic exists. However, what the author has offered the reader is an approach to analyzing acquisitions that will reduce the risk of overpaying for an acquisition. Risk is reduced because the analyses have adequately answered the executives' three basic questions concerning cost, return, and risk.

NOTES TO CHAPTER 8

[1]Paul B. Brown, "But, Frannie, They Do Own the Place," *Forbes*, June 4, 1984, pp. 180–82.

[2]Urban C. Lehner and Robert C. Simison, "GM to Acquire EDS in Transaction Valued at as Much as $2.55 Billion," *The Wall Street Journal*, June 29, 1984, p. 3

[3]Doron P. Levin, "Westinghouse Move into Robotics Shows Pitfalls of High-Tech Field," *The Wall Street Journal*, May 14, 1984.

Appendixes

Discounted Cash Flow
Techniques

A.1 INTRODUCTION

Throughout the book, calculations are performed that require an in-depth understanding of the **net present value (NPV)** and **internal rate of return (IRR)** methods of evaluating investment proposals. A brief review of these techniques is given here. (Note: This appendix should be skipped by those familiar with these techniques.)

Why should we use discounted cash flow (DCF) techniques to analyze target companies? Primarily, because an acquisition is similar to other typical capital expenditure proposals. It requires an outlay of funds or securities with a defined present cash value with the hope of receiving a greater cash flow stream in the future. The major factor differentiating analyzing an acquisition from other capital budgeting problems is its complexity—hundreds of assumptions are required to put together a realistic model of the expected cash flow stream. Nevertheless, the DCF methods that are used to analyze simple project proposals can still be properly used in acquisition analysis.

A.2 DCF THEORY

The theory underlying the use of DCF techniques is that a dollar received immediately is preferable to a dollar received at some future date. Why is this so? Because the dollar received today can be put to work and will be worth more than a dollar in the future.

EXAMPLE AA *ABC Corporation sells a product for $1,000. The buyer says that it would like to pay the $1,000 in one year. ABC Corporation can earn 9 percent by putting any excess cash in the bank. Marketing considerations aside, ABC Corporation would want the $1,000 now rather than later because if it gets the $1,000 now and invests it in the bank, it will have $1,090 at the end of a year versus $1,000 if it allows the customer to pay then.*

If a dollar today is worth more than a dollar at some future date, how does a person know when some future amount greater than a dollar is equal in value to a dollar today. In order to find this point, it is necessary to understand compounding and discounting. Virtually everyone has had experience with compound interest.

EXAMPLE AB *ABC Corporation puts $1,000 in a bank account earning 9 percent annually. At the end of three years ABC Corporation has $1,295 calculated as follows:*

Year	Initial Amount	Interest Rate	Period End Amount	Interest Received
1	$1,000	9%	$1,090	$ 90
2	1,090	9	1,188	98
3	1,188	9	1,295	107

The reason why the interest received in Years 2 and 3 exceeds 9 percent of the initial $1,000 is because ABC Corporation is receiving interest on previously earned interest.

Rather than set out the calculations necessary to find the compound value of $1, a table is provided in Illustration 1 that indicates what $1 will grow to over different periods using various compound interest rates.

Illustration 1
Compound Value of $1

Period	7%	8%	9%	10%	11%	12%	13%	14%	15%	16%
1	1.0700	1.0800	1.0900	1.1000	1.1100	1.1200	1.1300	1.1400	1.1500	1.1600
2	1.1449	1.1644	1.1881	1.2100	1.2321	1.2544	1.2769	1.2996	1.3225	1.3456
3	1.2250	1.2597	1.2950	1.3310	1.3676	1.4049	1.4429	1.4815	1.5209	1.5609
4	1.3108	1.3605	1.4116	1.4641	1.5181	1.5735	1.6305	1.6890	1.7490	1.8106
5	1.4026	1.4693	1.5386	1.6105	1.6851	1.7623	1.8424	1.9254	2.0114	2.1003
6	1.5007	1.5869	1.6771	1.7716	1.8704	1.9738	2.0820	2.1950	2.3131	2.4364
7	1.6058	1.7138	1.8280	2.9487	2.0762	2.2107	2.3526	2.5023	2.6600	2.8262
8	1.7182	1.8509	1.9926	2.1436	2.3045	2.4760	2.6584	2.8526	3.0590	3.2784
9	1.8385	1.9990	2.1719	2.3579	2.5580	2.7731	3.0040	3.2519	3.5179	3.8030
10	1.9672	2.1589	2.3674	2.5937	2.8394	3.1058	3.3946	3.7072	4.0456	4.4114

EXAMPLE AC *ABC Corporation puts $1,500 in the bank expecting to earn 14 percent compounded annually for five years. How much will ABC Corporation receive at the end of five years. If we look at the table above, we see that the factor for five periods at 14 percent is 1.9254. Multiplying $1,500 by 1.9254 we learn that ABC Corporation will receive $2,888 in five years.*

EXAMPLE AD *Same facts as Example AC except that ABC's money will be compounded semiannually. If this is the case, we look to the factor for 10 periods at 7 percent, which is 1.9672. Multiplying 1,500 by 1.9672 we see that ABC Corporation will receive $2,951 in five years.*

Discounting is the reverse of compounding. In discounting one is trying to find out what the value is today of a dollar at some point in the future.

EXAMPLE AE *ABC Corporation has a noninterest-bearing note receivable for $5,000 due in three years. Assume ABC will discount the note at 9 percent. If we look to the table above, we see that $1 will grow to $1.295 if it compounds at 9 percent for three years. Thus, the following relationships hold:*

$$\frac{1}{1.295} = \frac{X}{5,000}$$

Solving for X we find that the present value of $5,000 is $3,861.

Rather than have to continually solve for X, the table in Illustration 2 gives the factors that one can use to find the present value of $1. These factors were arrived at using the reciprocals of compound factors. In the example above we found the present value of $5,000 by solving for X. Instead of solving for X we could have just multiplied $5,000 by $\frac{1}{1.295}$ to get the answer. This fraction is the reciprocal of the compound value of $1 for three periods at 9 percent. It could otherwise be stated as .7722. Notice that this is the value that appears in the table in Illustration 2 for the present value of $1 discounted three periods at 9 percent.

Illustration 2
Present Value of $1

Period	7%	8%	9%	10%	11%	12%	13%	14%	15%	16%
1	.9346	.9259	.9174	.9091	.9009	.8929	.8850	.8772	.8696	.8621
2	.8734	.8573	.8417	.8264	.8116	.7972	.7831	.7695	.7561	.7432
3	.8163	.7938	.7722	.7513	.7312	.7118	.6931	.6750	.6575	.6407
4	.7629	.7350	.7084	.6830	.6587	.6355	.6133	.5921	.5718	.5523
5	.7130	.6806	.6499	.6209	.5935	.5674	.5428	.5194	.4972	.4761
6	.6663	.6302	.5963	.5645	.5346	.5066	.4803	.4556	.4323	.4104
7	.6227	.5835	.5470	.5132	.4817	.4523	.4251	.3996	.3759	.3538
8	.5820	.5403	.5019	.4665	.4339	.4039	.3762	.3506	.3269	.3050
9	.5439	.5002	.4604	.4241	.3909	.3606	.3329	.3075	.2843	.2630
10	.5083	.4632	.4224	.3855	.3522	.3220	.2946	.2697	.2472	.2267

EXAMPLE AF *ABC Corporation will receive $10,000 in five years and wants to determine its present value using a 10 percent discount factor. Looking at the table, the discount factor for five periods at 10 percent is .6209. Multiplying $10,000 by this factor we find that the present value of the sum to be received is $6,209.*

EXAMPLE AG *ABC Corporation expects to receive cash at the end of each of the next four years. The cash flows are as indicated below. Using a 12 percent discount factor, what is the present value of these cash flows?*

Period	Cash Flow	12 Percent Discount Factor	Present Value
1	$ 700	.8929	$ 625
2	1,225	.7972	977
3	1,943	.7118	1,383
4	420	.6355	267
Total cash flow	$4,288	Total present value	$3,252

A.3 NET PRESENT VALUE METHOD

The NPV method involves discounting the net cash flows expected from a project at a single discount rate and subtracting from it the initial cost of the project. Most financial authors take the position that the discount rate to be used in performing the calculation is the company's weighted-average cost of capital. However, many corporations annually fix cutoff returns (the discount rate) for approving capital projects. The investment rule to apply with the NPV method is that if the NPV is a positive number, the project should be undertaken; whereas if it is negative, the project should be dropped.

EXAMPLE AH *XYZ Corporation is looking at buying ABC Corporation for $10 million. XYZ expects net cash flows from the acquisition as stated below. XYZ's cutoff rate of return is 13 percent. Should XYZ buy ABC?*

Year	Net Cash Flow	13 Percent Discount Rate	Net Present Value
1	$1,000	.8850	$ 885
2	3,833	.7831	3,002
3	3,800	.6931	2,634
4	6,400	.6133	3,925
5	670	.5428	364
		Present value of cash flows	10,810
		Less: Acquisition cost	10,000
		Net present value	$ 810

Answer *Yes, XYZ should buy ABC Corporation because the project has a positive net present value.*

A.4   INTERNAL RATE OF RETURN METHOD

The IRR method is defined as the interest rate that makes the present value of the expected net cash flows equal to the cost of the project. The investment rule to follow is that a project should be accepted if its IRR exceeds the cutoff rate of return set by management.

EXAMPLE AI   *Same facts as Example AH. What is the internal rate of return?*

Year	Net Cash Flow	16 Percent Discount Rate*	Net Present Value
1	$1,000	.8621	$ 862
2	3,833	.7432	2,849
3	3,800	.6407	2,435
4	6,400	.5523	3,535
5	670	.4761	319
		Present value of cash flows	10,000
		Less: Acquisition cost	(10,000)
		Net present value	$ 0

*The 16 percent discount rate can be found using the trial and error method or by using most calculators or computers.

   Answer   *XYZ should buy ABC because the project has an internal rate of return (16 percent) which exceeds XYZ Corporation's weighted-average cost of capital.*

A.5   WHICH METHOD IS PREFERABLE?

Under normal circumstances the two method will give the same results. However, it is important to understand that the two methods are based on different reinvestment assumptions. The NPV method assumes that all proceeds can be reinvested at the firm's cutoff return or weighted-average cost of capital, whichever is the discount rate used. The IRR method assumes that all proceeds can be reinvested at the internal rate of return. In most cases the NPV assumption is the better assumption. Furthermore, there can be practical problems with the IRR method because in certain instances several internal rates of return can exist for a project. In the typical project there is one cash outflow in period 1 followed thereafter by cash receipts. In this situation only one IRR is generated. However, if there are cash outflows in more than one period, multiple IRR's can be generated. In these cases the NPV method should be used to analyze the project.

Despite the shortcomings of the IRR method, it is used extensively in Sections Three and Four. Why? Because the key to successful acquisition negotiations depends on giving the chief negotiator (who is often not a financial person) as much information as possible about the transaction in a highly intelligible form. The IRR method is preferred over the NPV method because it results in a percentage figure which executives readily understand. However, the NPV method is also extremely useful and illustrative in certain areas. The cost analysis draws extensively on this method.

REFERENCES FOR APPENDIX A

Brealey, Richard, and Stewart Myers. *Principles of Corporate Finance*, 10–110. New York: McGraw-Hill, 1981.

Brigham, Eugene F. *Financial Management Theory and Practice*, 2d ed., 39–95, 351–402. Hinsdale, Ill.: The Dryden Press, 1979.

Copeland, Thomas E., and J. Fred Weston. *Financial Theory and Corporate Policy*, 15–41. Reading, Mass: Addison-Wesley Publishing Company, 1980.

Weston, J. Fred, and Eugene F. Brigham. *Essentials of Managerial Finance*, 3d ed., 213–70. Hinsdale, Ill.: The Dryden Press, 1974.

Wright, M. G. *Discounted Cash Flow*, 2d ed., 1–81. Maidenhead, England: McGraw-Hill Book Co. (UK) Ltd., 1973.

Basic Tax Rules

B.1   INTRODUCTION

In order to comprehend the analyses described in this book, it is necessary to have a firm grasp on some basic tax concepts. These concepts include the present corporate tax rate structure, taxation of capital gains and losses at both the shareholder and corporate levels, depreciation rules, the tax credit program associated with certain investments, LIFO recapture rules, and net operating losses.

B.2   CORPORATE ORDINARY INCOME TAX RATES

The ordinary corporate income tax rate is 46 percent. However, corporations with taxable income less than $1 million receive the benefit of a graduated rate structure on the first $100,000 of taxable income.[1] This rate structure, which follows, produces a maximum tax savings of $20,250.

Taxable Income	Rate
$ 0–$ 25,000	15%
25,001– 50,000	18
50,001– 75,000	30
75,001– 100,000	40
100,000 and up	46

EXAMPLE BA   *ABC has taxable income in 1984 of $200,000 and no credits. What is its tax due?*

EXAMPLE BA

	$ 25,000	×	15%	=	$ 3,750
	25,000	×	18%	=	4,500
	25,000	×	30%	=	7,500
	25,000	×	40%	=	10,000
	100,000	×	46%	=	46,000
Taxable income	$200,000			Tax due =	$71,750

The benefit of the graduated rate structure is phased out for companies with taxable income in excess of $1 million through the imposition of an additional tax. This tax is equal to the lesser of $20,250 or 5 percent of taxable income in excess of $1 million.

EXAMPLE BB   *ABC Corporation has taxable income in 1984 of $1,350,000. What is its tax due?*

		Tax
1st $100,000 of taxable income		$ 25,750
Next 1,250,000 of taxable income		575,000
		600,750
Additional tax		
Taxable income	$1,350,000	
Exempt amount	(1,000,000)	
Excess	350,000	
Tax rate	5%	
		17,500
Total tax owed		$ 618,250

It is important to note that throughout this book we assume an ordinary income tax rate of 50 percent, which in light of the combined federal and state tax structures is reasonable.

B.3   CAPITAL GAINS AND LOSSES

Gain on the sale or exchange of a capital asset that has been held for the required holding period is taxed at a lower rate than the ordinary tax rate. However, gain on the sale of a capital asset held for less than the required holding period is subject to tax at the ordinary income tax rates.

B.301   Required Holding Period

The present required holding period for taxing capital gain at a lower rate is six months.[2] The gain or loss on the sale of an asset meeting the holding period requirement is called a long-term capital gain or loss. If the holding period requirement is not met, the gain or loss is short term.

B.302 Capital Assets Defined

A capital asset is defined as property (whether or not connected with a trade or business) held by the taxpayer, but which does not include (1) inventory, (2) accounts receivable, (3) depreciable business property, (4) real property used in a trade or business, and (5) some miscellaneous other assets.[3]

B.303 Section 1231 Assets

The definition of capital assets specifically excludes real property and depreciable property used in a business. This exclusion drastically curtails the opportunity to sell all the assets of a business and be taxed on any gain at the capital gains rate. However, Section 1231 alleviates the problem for the taxpayer. Under Section 1231, gains and losses on property used in a trade or business (which includes real property, depreciable business property and certain other items) are netted together. If the gains exceed the losses, both the gains and losses shall be considered as arising from the sale or exchange of a capital asset held for the required holding period. However, if the losses exceed the gains, the net loss will be offset against other taxable income which is taxed at the ordinary tax rate. The net effect of this provision is that the taxpayer gets the best of both worlds; he is taxed at capital gains rates if there are gains, yet he gets an ordinary loss deduction if there are losses.

EXAMPLE BC *ABC Corporation sells all of its assets. All assets have been held for the required holding period. These assets include certain Section 1231 assets listed below. We will disregard any depreciation recapture in this example.*

	Tax Basis	*Fair Market Value per Contract*	*Recognized Gains*
Land	$ 50,000	$ 60,000	$ 10,000
Building	140,000	200,000	60,000
Machinery	200,000	250,000	50,000
		Net recognized gain	$120,000

Since there is a net gain on Section 1231 items, the taxpayer will treat all gains and losses as if they arose from the sale of a capital asset that had been held for the required holding period.

However, the benefit afforded by Section 1231 cannot be manipulated through the judicious timing of transactions to produce gains or losses in selected years. Net Section 1231 gain will be treated as ordinary income to the extent that the sum of net Section 1231 gains and losses for the previous five years is a loss.

B.304 Interplay of Section 1231 with Depreciation Recapture Provisions

The Section 1231 gain on the sale or exchange of real property and depreciable property used in a trade or business is computed by deducting the depreciation recaptured under sections 1245 and 1250 from the total gain.[4] Depreciation recapture is discussed in detail later in this appendix (see paragraph B.405).

EXAMPLE BD   *Same facts as Example BC except that there is depreciation recapture under Section 1250 of $20,000 relating to the building and depreciation recapture under Section 1245 of $30,000 relating to the machinery.*

	Recognized Gain	*Depreciation Recapture*	*Section 1231 Gain*
Land	$ 10,000		$10,000
Building	60,000	$20,000	40,000
Machinery	50,000	30,000	20,000
	$120,000	$50,000	$70,000

ABC Corporation will treat the $70,000 gain as if it arose from the sale of a capital asset and will have $50,000 ordinary income under the recapture provisions (see paragraph B.405).

B.305 Computation of Tax on Capital Gains and Losses

The first step in determining the tax on the sale of capital assets is to net (*a*) all long-term capital gains with long-term capital losses and (*b*) all short-term capital gains with all short-term capital losses. Having done this, the long-term gains or losses are then netted with the short-term gains or losses as shown in Illustration 1.

The taxation of the alternatives varies depending on whether the taxpayer is an individual or a corporation. (Note: In the discussion below, the terms net long-/short-term gains/losses refer to column 3.)

Illustration 1

(1) Net Long-Term Gain or Loss Alternatives		*(2)* Net Short-Term Gain or Loss Alternatives		*(3)* Alternative Results	Alter- native Number
Any net long-term gain	+	Any Net short-term gain	=	Net long-term gain + Net short-term gain	1
Larger net long-term gain	+	Smaller net short-term loss	=	Net long-term gain	2
Smaller net Long-term loss	+	Larger net short-term gain	=	Net short-term gain	3
Smaller net Long-term gain	+	Larger net short-term loss	=	Net short-term loss	4
Any net long-term loss	+	Any net short-term loss	=	Net long term loss + Net short-term loss	5
Larger net long-term loss	+	Smaller net short-term gain	=	Net long-term loss	6

B.305a *Individuals*

An individual may deduct from gross income 60 percent of the amount of the net long-term capital gain in alternative number 1 or net long-term capital gain in alternative number 2. The remaining 40 percent is included in gross income.[5]

EXAMPLE BE   *John Doe has a net long-term capital gain of $10,000 and a net short-term capital gain of $5,000. John Doe will exclude $6,000 ($10,000 × 60%) of the net long-term capital gain from gross income.*

In alternative 3 where an individual has a net short-term gain, the taxpayer merely includes this net gain in gross income. If an individual has a net short-term capital loss as in alternative 4 or a net long-term loss and a net short-term loss as in alternative 5, the taxpayer may offset the net short-term loss against other taxable income up to a $3,000 annual limitation. If the net short-term loss exceeds the limitation, the excess short-term loss may be carried over. If the net short-term loss does not exceed the limitation in alternative 5, then one half of the net long-term capital loss may also be deducted, subject to the $3,000 annual total limitation.[6]

EXAMPLE BF   *John Doe has a net short-term capital loss of $2,000 and a net long-term capital loss of $4,000. John Doe may apply the $2,000 of short-term capital losses against other income because it is under the limitation. Furthermore, John Doe may deduct another $2,000 of long-term capital losses to reach the $3,000 limitation.*

Net short-term capital losses	$2,000
Net long-term capital losses ($2,000 × 1/2)	1,000
Total applied against other taxable income	$3,000

John Doe also has a long-term capital loss carryforward of $2,000.

Finally, if the taxpayer has a net long-term loss as in alternative 6, the taxpayer may deduct one half of the net loss against other taxable income up to the $3,000 limitation and carryforward any excess.

B.305b Corporations

A corporation will include the amount of net long-term capital gain in alternatives 1 and 2 in gross income, and a tax at the regular corporate rates will be computed. However, an alternative tax is also computed by calculating a tax on the corporation's taxable income excluding the net long-term capital gains and adding to the tax calculated an amount equal to 28 percent of the net long-term capital gains. The corporation will use the calculation that yields the lower total tax.[7] (See also paragraph B.10.)

EXAMPLE BG *ABC Corporation has other taxable income of $100,000, net long-term capital gains of $50,000, and net short-term capital gains of $100,000. We will assume that the ordinary corporate tax rate is a flat 46 percent. ABC Corporation will pay the $106,000 due under the alternative calculation.*

Regular Calculation

Other taxable income	$100,000	
Net short-term capital gains	100,000	
Net long-term capital gains	50,000	
	250,000	
Ordinary tax rate	× 46%	
Tax at ordinary rate	$115,000	

Alternative Tax Calculation

Other taxable income	$100,000	
Net short-term capital gains	100,000	
	200,000	
Ordinary tax rate	× 46%	
Tax at ordinary rate	$ 92,000	$ 92,000
Net long-term capital gains	$ 50,000	
Capital gains tax rate	× 28%	
Capital gains tax	$ 14,000	14,000
Total alternative tax		$106,000

In alternative 3 where a corporation has a net short-term capital gain, the taxpayer merely includes the net gain in gross income. In alternatives 4, 5, and 6, a corporation cannot offset capital losses against current ordinary income. The corporation can only carryback or carryforward the losses and apply them against capital gains. All losses carried back or carried over are treated as short-term capital losses.

B.306 Individual Net Capital Loss Carryover

Individuals may carryover net capital losses for an indefinite time period until they are used up. Losses carried over retain their character as either long term or short term.[8]

B.307 Corporate Capital Loss Carryback/Carryover

Corporations may carryback a net capital loss to any of the three preceding taxable years or carryforward the loss to any of the subsequent five taxable years. If the capital losses are not used in the next five years, they are lost as deductions. Capital losses carried back or carried over can only be offset against capital gains.[9]

B.4 DEPRECIATION RULES

Depreciation of assets in the 1980s is generally governed by three sets of rules. Which set of rules is appropriate for a particular asset depends on when an asset was placed in service. The following table lists the governing rules and time periods for when an asset was placed in service.

Applicable Rules	*Assets Placed in Service*
Accelerated Cost Recovery System (ACRS)	1981 and therafter
Class Life ADR System (CLADR)	1971–80
Class Life System (CLS)	Prior to 1971

B.401 ACRS

The ACRS was enacted by Congress in 1981 to provide an incentive for capital investment. This system was a radical departure from prior depreciation systems and simplified the depreciation rules significantly.[10] ACRS applies to all recovery property that is placed in service. Recovery property is defined as tangible property of a character subject to the allowance for depreciation that is used in a trade or business or held for the production of income. Practically speaking, this definition covers most assets with some major exceptions being intangible assets, land, and assets subject to depletion allowances. Property is placed in service when it is ready and available for a specifically assigned function.

B.401a   Classes of Recovery Property

Each item of recovery property is assigned to one of six classes.[11]

A. 3-Year Property. Personal property and other tangible property (not including a building or its structural components) used as an integral part of manufacturing production, extraction or the furnishing of utility-like services that has a present class life of four years or less or is used in connection with research and experimentation. This class of property would include automobiles, trucks, and certain specified devices used in manufacture. The concept of present class life mentioned above is used to link key recovery periods to prior law asset guideline periods (see paragraphs B.403a and B.404).

B. 5-Year Property. All personal property and other tangible property (not including a building or its structural components) used as an integral part of manufacturing, production, extraction, or the furnishing of utility-like service that are not included in the 3-year class. This class would include most machinery and equipment and single-purpose agricultural and storage structures.

C. 10-Year Property. This class includes certain public utility property, real property with a present class life of 12.5 years or less, theme and amusement park structures, railroad tank cars, and miscellaneous other items.

D. 15-Year Real Property. This class included all real property not included in another class (e.g., buildings, components, and improvements) which was placed in service prior to March 15, 1984. Presently it only includes low income housing reality.

E. 15-Year Public Utility Property. This class includes all public utility property other than real property, 3-year property, and public utility property included in the 10-year property class. It includes electric, gas, water, and telephone utility plants.

F. 18-Year Real Property. This class includes all real property not included in another class (e.g., buildings, components, and improvements) which was placed in service after March 15, 1984.

B.401b   Amount of Depreciation Deduction

The amount of the depreciation deduction for any year is determined by multiplying the tax basis (generally cost) of the asset by the applicable percentage given in Illustrations 2, 3 and 4.[12]

In calculating the depreciation deduction for recovery property placed in service subsequent to 1982, the basis of such property must first be reduced by one half the regular investment tax credit if the full investment tax credit is taken (but see paragraph B.507).

Illustration 2

If the Recovery Year Is:	The Applicable Percentage for the Class of Property Is:			
	3-Year	*5-Year*	*10-Year*	*15-Year Public Utility*
1	25	15	8	5
2	38	22	14	10
3	37	21	12	9
4		21	10	8
5		21	10	7
6			10	7
7			9	6
8			9	6
9			9	6
10			9	6
11				6
12				6
13				6
14				6
15				6

The 1984 Tax Reform Act requires that the IRS provide a new rate table for 18-year real property. This table is to be constructed assuming that real property is placed in service in the middle of the month. The IRS has not published this table at the date of this writing. However, Illustration 4 indicates the depreciation rates that can be expected (rounded to the nearest percent).

B.401c   Straight-Line Election
A taxpayer may prefer a slower recovery of cost in certain instances. The Code provides for an election of the straight-line method. If a taxpayer makes such an election, recovery periods are dictated as follows:[13]

Class of Property	*Straight-Line Recovery Period Alternatives*
3-year property	3, 5, or 12 years
5-year property	5, 12, or 25 years
10-year property	10, 25, or 35 years
15-year real property	15, 35, or 45 years
15-year public utility property	15, 35, or 45 years

Illustration 3

If the Recovery Year Is:	The Applicable Percentage for 15-Year Real Property Is:											
	Month of Taxable Year That Asset Is Placed in Service											
	1	2	3	4	5	6	7	8	9	10	11	12
1	12	11	10	9	8	7	6	5	4	3	2	1
2	10	10	11	11	11	11	11	11	11	11	11	10
3	9	9	9	9	10	10	10	10	10	10	10	10
4	8	8	8	8	8	8	9	9	9	9	9	9
5	7	7	7	7	7	7	8	8	8	8	8	8
6	6	6	6	6	6	7	7	7	7	7	7	7
7	6	6	6	6	6	6	6	6	6	6	6	6
8	6	6	6	6	6	6	6	6	6	6	6	6
9	6	6	6	6	5	6	5	6	6	6	6	6
10	5	5	5	5	5	5	5	5	5	5	5	5
11	5	5	5	5	5	5	5	5	5	5	5	5
12	5	5	5	5	5	5	5	5	5	5	5	5
13	5	5	5	5	5	5	5	5	5	5	5	5
14	5	5	5	5	5	5	5	5	5	5	5	5
15	5	5	5	5	5	5	5	5	5	5	5	5
16			1	1	2	2	3	3	4	4	4	5

Note: This table does not apply to low-income housing.

Illustration 4

Year	Applicable Percentage for 18-Year Real Property Placed in Service January 1
1	9
2	9
3	8
4	7
5	6
6	6
7	5
8	5
9	5
10	5
11	5
12	5
13	5
14	4
15	4
16	4
17	4
18	4

Generally, a straight-line election applies to all property in the class to which the election applies. However, for 15-year real property the straight-line election can be made on a property by property basis.

B.402   Old Depreciation Systems

The purpose of this appendix is to outline the key tax concepts that affect the acquisition pricing decision. The older depreciation systems are important only in instances where the acquiring company will acquire the target company in a manner that will result in the carryover of the target company's tax attributes. Therefore, a detailed analysis of the older depreciation systems is unnecessary. Discussion can be limited to how depreciation is calculated today on assets placed in service under these old systems.[14]

The starting point for calculating depreciation under the old methods is the tax basis (cost) of the asset. Salvage value, which is the amount a taxpayer expects to receive upon disposition of the asset at the end of its useful life, also plays an important role in the depreciation calculations. Generally, one computes depreciation by using certain approved methods within the framework of the useful life of a particular asset. The useful life of an asset is determined within the guidelines set forth by the depreciation system.

B.403   Class Life Asset Depreciation Range (CLADR) System

The CLADR System is used for depreciating assets placed in service after 1970 but before 1981. This system applies to all tangible personal property and real property that has a class and a class life. Under this system if salvage value is 10 percent or less, an election could be made to ignore salvage value in calculating depreciation.

B.403a   Classifying Assets

The CLADR System provides for separate classes for most types of assets. Each class has a stated useful life and possibly a range of useful lives that are used in calculating depreciation deductions for assets in that class. In situations where a class has a range of useful lives, a taxpayer can select any useful life that is within the range.

B.403b   Permissible Methods

The specifically authorized depreciation methods under the CLADR System include (*a*) straight line, (*b*) sum-of-the-years' digits, or (*c*) any acceptable double-declining-balance method. However, any reasonable method of computing depreciation is permissible so long as it is consistently applied.

a. Straight-Line Method. Depreciation is calculated by reducing the basis by the salvage value and dividing the remainder by the useful life.

EXAMPLE BH   *Tangible personal property costs $5,000, has a five-year useful life, and $100 salvage value, which is ignored since it is under 10 percent of cost. Annual depreciation under the straight-line method would be ($5,000/5) = $1,000.*

b. Sum-of-the-Years'-Digits Method. In order to calculate depreciation under this method, the years of an asset's useful life must first be totaled. The deduction is figured by multiplying the assets basis (less salvage value if it exceeds 10 percent of cost) by a fraction; the numerator of which is the remaining useful life at the beginning of the year, and the denominator is the sum-of-the-year's digits. This method can only be used for new tangible assets with a useful life of three years or more.

EXAMPLE BI   *Assume the same facts as Example BH except that the sum-of-the-years'-digits method is used.*

		Depreciation Deduction
1st year	($5,000 × 5/15)	$1,687
2d year	($5,000 × 4/15)	1,334
3d year	($5,000 × 3/15)	1,000
4th year	($5,000 × 2/15)	666
5th year	($5,000 × 1/15)	333
	Total	$5,000

c. Declining-Balance Method. The depreciation deduction is calculated by multiplying the asset's tax basis, reduced by all previously deducted depreciation, by the appropriate declining-balance rate. The declining-balance rates are all expressed as a percentage of straight-line rates. The maximum declining-balance rates that may be used are:

Type of Property	Maximum Declining-Balance Rate
New tangible personal property	200%
Used tangible personal property	150
Real property	150

EXAMPLE BJ *Same facts as Example BI except that the 200 percent declining-balance method is used. Under straight-line depreciation the annual depreciation rate would be 20 percent, so using the 200 percent declining-balance method the rate is 40 percent.*

Year	Remaining Basis	Declining-Balance Rate	Depreciation Allowance
1	$5,000	40%	$2,000
2	3,000	40	1,200
3	1,800	40	720
4	1,080	40	432
5	648	40	259
		Total	$4,611

It is obvious that this method does not completely depreciate the asset over its useful life. Therefore, in order to maximize their tax deductions, companies change methods to straight-line depreciation at the point where the straight-line method yields a larger deduction than the declining-balance method.

B.404   Class Life System (CLS)

When the CLADR System was adopted, the Treasury also provided for an elective CLS for calculating depreciation deductions in 1971 and later years on assets placed in service prior to 1971. This system generally operates in the same manner as the CLADR System except that under CLS there are no ranges within each class of assets. Therefore, an asset falling within a particular class must be depreciated based on a singular useful life, technically known as the asset guideline period, for that class.

B.405 Depreciation Recapture

The depreciation recapture provisions were enacted in order to tax at ordinary rates rather than capital gains rates all or a portion of the gain on the sale of certain property. There are two sets of rules governing depreciation recapture: (1) rules for recovery property that apply to property placed in service under ACRS provisions and (2) rules for property placed in service prior to 1981, which is when the ACRS rules became effective. Both sets of rules are embodied in Sections 1245 and 1250. The most important differences in the two sets of rules are the definitions of what constitutes Section 1245 and 1250 property.

B.405a Rules for Recovery Property

The recapture rules under Section 1245 apply to all recovery property except (1) residential rental property, (2) property used predominantly outside the United States, (3) 18-year or 15-year real property for which a straight-line election is made under ACRS rules, and (4) miscellaneous other property.[15] Under Section 1245 the gain on the sale of Section 1245 recovery property is taxed as ordinary income to the extent of all ACRS deductions.

EXAMPLE BK   *ABC Corporation sells certain of its assets that are listed below. At the time the assets were placed in service (January 1982), no straight-line election was made with respect to any of the assets (see paragraph B.401c).*

	Current Tax Basis	Accumulated ACRS Deductions	Contract Sale Price	Section 1245 Recapture Income
Buildings and improvements	$30,000	$35,000	$ 60,000	$30,000
Manufacturing machinery	45,000	20,000	100,000	20,000
Packaging machinery	25,000	75,000	25,000	–0–
	Total Section 1245 recapture income			$50,000

The effect of not making a straight-line election with respect to the plant's building and improvements, which for ACRS purposes is classified as 15-year real property, is to cause a large amount of depreciation deductions ($30,000) to be recaptured. If ABC Corporation had elected straight-line depreciation for the building and improvements, no depreciation deductions for buildings and improvements would have been recaptured.

A sound rule for management to follow in deciding whether or not to opt for straight-line depreciation for 18-year or 15-year real property is: "Never take ACRS depreciation deductions for 18-year or 15-year real property if management believes there is any real probability that the property will be sold in the foreseeable future."

Under Section 1250 the gain on the sale of (1) residential rental property, (2) property used predominantly outside of the United States, (3) 18-year or 15-year real property for which a straight-line election is made under ACRS rules, and (4) miscellaneous other property is taxed at ordinary income rates only to the extent that the depreciation deductions taken exceed the depreciation deductions allowable using the straight-line depreciation method.

EXAMPLE BL   *ABC Corporation sells its only asset on January 1, 1985, for $126,000. This asset is residential rental property that was originally placed in service on January 1, 1983, at a cost of $100,000 (assume that the cost relates 100 percent to Section 1250 property). The asset has a current tax basis of $78,000. If the straight-line election had been made, only $13,333 of depreciation deductions would have been taken. Therefore, the difference between the $22,000 depreciation deductions taken and $13,333 ($8,667) is recaptured as ordinary income under Section 1250, and $39,333 is treated as capital gain under Section 1231.*

B.405b   Rules for Assets Placed in Service Prior to 1981

The rules for assets placed in service prior to 1981 are also included in various provisions of Sections 1245 and 1250. Assets are defined, for depreciation recapture purposes, as either Section 1245 property or Section 1250 property. Section 1245 property is defined generally as personal property and other tangible property (not including a building or its structural components) used as an integral part of manufacturing, production, extraction, the furnishing of utility-like services, and other miscellaneous uses. Section 1250 property is defined as any real property that is a of a character subject to depreciation that is not Section 1245 property.

Section 1245 Property.   Generally gain on the sale of Section 1245 property placed in service prior to 1981 is taxed as ordinary income to the extent of all depreciation and amortization taken since 1961.

EXAMPLE BM   *ABC Corporation purchased a Section 1245 asset and placed it in service in 1975 at a cost of $150,000. For the years 1975–84, the taxpayer took $110,000 of depreciation deductions. On January 1, 1985, the taxpayer sells the asset for $75,000. The taxpayer has ordinary income due to depreciation recapture of $35,000 ($75,000–$40,000), which is the sale price less the tax basis. If the taxpayer had sold the asset for $200,000, there would have been $110,000 of ordinary income and $50,000 of Section 1231 gain.*

Section 1250 Property.   Generally gain on the sale of Section 1250 property is taxed as ordinary income to the extent that depreciation deductions after 1965 exceed the straight-line deductions that would have been allowed.

B.5 INVESTMENT TAX CREDIT

The investment tax credit provisions of the Code were enacted by Congress to stimulate the purchase of certain types of assets. These provisions accomplish their objective by providing for a credit against a taxpayer's federal income tax liability that is equal to a percentage of the amount the taxpayer spends for certain property.

B.501 Basic Credit Percentages

Generally, the credit is computed at the basic rate of 10 percent of the qualified investment.[16] However, for the period January 22, 1975, through December 31, 1982, a corporate taxpayer was entitled to an additional one percent credit if an amount equal to 1 percent of the qualified investment was contributed to an employee stock ownership plan (ESOP). Furthermore, another 1/2 percent credit could be claimed if the taxpayer contributed an additional 1/2 percent to the ESOP which was matched by the employees.[17] The ESOP credit was replaced after December 31, 1982, with a payroll based tax credit. The amount of the credit is based on the lesser of—

1. The aggregate value of employer securities transferred to the tax credit employee stock ownership plan, or
2. The applicable percentage (1/2 percent through 1987) of the amount of the aggregate compensation paid to all employees under a tax credit employee stock ownership plan.[18]

B.502 Qualified Property

Property used exclusively for business purposes, eligible for the investment credit is technically known as "Section 38 Property." Such property includes (*a*) depreciable tangible personal property such as machinery, equipment, and automobiles; and (*b*) depreciable real property excluding buildings and their structural components) that is used as an integral part of manufacturing, production, extraction, or the furnishing of utility like services.[19]

B.503 Computation of Credit

A taxpayer's credit is determined by calculating the qualified investment in Section 38 Property (exclusive of any listed property) and multiplying this amount by the appropriate credit percentage. There are two sets of rules governing a taxpayer's qualified investment: (*a*) old rules for 1980 and prior years and (*b*) new rules for 1981 and thereafter.

Old rules. Under these rules the qualified investment in new Section 38 Property was equal to the taxpayer's basis (cost to place the asset in service) multiplied times the applicable percentage described below.[20]

If the Asset's Useful Life Is:	The Applicable Percentage Is:
3–5 years	33⅓
5–7 years	66⅔
7 or more years	100

EXAMPLE BN   *B Corporation purchased the following in 1979:*

Section 38 Asset	Useful Life	Cost	Applicable Percentage	Qualified Investment
Machine A	10 years	$200	100	$200
Machine B	6 years	900	66⅔	600
Automobile	3 years	300	33⅓	100
		Subtotal		900
		Credit percentage		10%
		Investment tax credit		$ 90

New rules. Under the new rules the qualified investment in new Section 38 Property is equal to the taxpayers basis multiplied times the applicable percentage described below.[21]

Class of Property	Applicable Percentage
3-year property	60
5-year property	100
10-year property	100
15-year public utility property	100

EXAMPLE BO   *B Corporation purchased the following in 1984:*

Section 38 Asset	Class of Property	Cost	Applicable Percentage	Qualified Investment
Machine A	5-year	$200	100	$ 200
Machine B	5-year	900	100	900
Automobile	3-year	300	60	180
		Subtotal		1,280
		Credit percentage		10%
		Investment tax credit		$ 128

Remember, if a taxpayer elects to take the full investment tax credit on an asset, the tax basis of the asset will be reduced for purposes of computing the allowable depreciation deductions (see paragraphs B.401b and B.507).

B.504 Used Section 38 Property

A taxpayer's qualified investment in used Section 38 Property cannot exceed $125,000.[22] The practical result of this law is to limit the investment tax credit in the context of a business acquisition to $12,500—a relatively insignificant figure in most acquisitions.

B.505 Limitation on Credit

A taxpayer adds its investment tax credit (both regular and the energy credits), targeted jobs credit, alcohol fuels credit, and the ESOP credit into one general business credit. The general business credit can be applied against the first $25,000 of net tax liability plus 85 percent of the net tax liability over $25,000.[23] The taxpayer's net tax liability equals the taxpayer's income tax liability reduced by various taxes (e.g., corporate minimum tax, accumulated earnings tax) and credits (e.g., foreign tax credit, incremental research expense credit).

EXAMPLE BP *B Corporation has a net tax liability of $125,000, current general business tax credits of $120,000, and no carryover tax credits.*

		Credit Limitation
Tax liability	$125,000	
Excess tax liability	−25,000	$ 25,000
	100,000	
	85%	
	$ 85,000	85,000
Total credit limitation		$110,000
General business tax credits		$120,000
General business tax credits allowance		$110,000
General business tax credit carryback/carryover		$ 10,000

B.506 Carryback and Carryover of Unused Credits

If the credit cannot be utilized because of the limitation described in the preceding paragraph, it can be carried back to each of the 3 preceding years or carried over for the next 15 years.[24] The order in which credits are used up follows a first-in, first-out approach.

EXAMPLE BQ   *In Example BP if B Corporation had a "net tax liability" of $30,000 in the preceding year against which no credits were claimed, B Corporation could carryback the $10,000 credit and obtain a refund.*

B.507   Credit Reduction Election

The general rule, as stated in paragraph B.401b, is that a taxpayer must reduce the basis of property placed in service subsequent to 1982 by one half the regular investment tax credit. However, instead of reducing an asset's basis for depreciation purposes, a taxpayer may alternatively elect to reduce the regular investment tax credit by 2 percent as described below.[25] If such an election is made, no reduction is made in calculating depreciation deductions. (See Illustration 5.) This election can be made on a property by property basis.

Illustration 5

		General Rule				Election
				Investment	Effective	Reduced
		Applicable	Qualified	Tax Credit	ITC	ITC
Class of Property	Cost	Percentage	Investment	Percentage	Percentage	Percentage
3-year	$100	60	$ 60	10	6	4
5-year	100	100	100	10	10	8
10-year	100	100	100	10	10	8
15-year public utility	100	100	100	10	10	8

B.508   Recapture of Investment Tax Credit

If Section 38 Property is disposed of before the end of its useful life or recapture period, then the tax liability in the year of disposal is increased by the amount of the credit that is recaptured. Both an Asset Acquisition or a 338 Transaction (see paragraph 3.202) qualify as dispositions which will trigger the recapture of investment tax credits. Separate recapture percentages are provided in Illustrations 6 and 7 for Section 38 Property placed in service under the old and new rules.

EXAMPLE BR   *B Corporation purchases the following assets as indicated and sells all of its assets on October 15, 1984:*

Asset	Date Purchased	Useful Life	Class of Property	ITC Taken	Recapture Percentage	ITC Tax Recapture
Machine A	1/1/79	8		$300	33 1/3	$100
Machine B	1/1/77	6		700	0	0
Machine C	1/1/80	6		500	50	250
Automobile	1/1/81		3-year	200	0	0
Machine D	1/1/82		5-year	50	60	30
				Total ITC recapture		$380

Illustration 6
Recapture Percentages for Property Placed in Service under Old Rules[26]

Number of Full Years of Service	*The Recapture Percentage for Property With an Original Useful Life of—*		
	3–5 Years	*5–7 Years*	*7+ Years*
0	100	100	100
1	100	100	100
2	100	100	100
3		50	66.6
4		50	66.6
5			33.3
6			33.3

Illustration 7
Recapture Percentages for Property Placed in Service under New Rules[27]

Number of Full Years of Service	*The Recapture Percentage for—*	
	3-Year Property	*5-, 10-, and 15-Year Property*
0	100	100
1	66	80
2	33	60
3		40
4		20

B.6 BUSINESS ENERGY CREDIT

In an effort to stimulate investment in alternate energy sources, Congress passed legislation in 1978 providing for additional tax credits for those taxpayers who invested in favored alternate energy projects.

B.601 Basic Credit Percentages

The favored investments, the credits provided, and the applicable time periods for the credits are detailed in Illustration 8.[28]

Illustration 8

Property Description	Energy Percentage	Period
General rule for energy not described below	10	10/1/78 to 12/31/82 (or to 12/31/90 for certain long-term projects)
Solar, wind or geothermal property	10	10/1/78 to 12/31/79
	15	1/1/80 to 12/31/85
Ocean thermal property	15	1/1/80 to 12/31/85
Qualified hydroelectric	11	1/1/80 to 12/31/85 (or to 12/31/88 for certain such property)
Qualified intercity buses	10	1/1/80 to 12/31/85
Biomass property	10	10/1/78 to 12/31/85

B.602   Qualified Property

Property does not have to be Section 38 Property to qualify for the energy investment credit. However, if property is Section 38 Property, it qualifies for both the regular investment credit and the business energy investment credit.

B.603   Computation of Credit

The qualified investment is determined in the same manner as the qualified investment for the regular investment tax credit.

B.7   LIFO RECAPTURE

A company that sells inventory valued using the LIFO method in the course of a 337 Liquidation must recognize as ordinary income the "LIFO (last-in, first-out) Recapture Amount." The **LIFO Recapture Amount** is equal to the excess of the adjusted basis of the inventory under the FIFO (first-in, first-out) method over its LIFO adjusted basis.

EXAMPLE BS   *ABC Corporation sells all of its assets to XYZ Corporation in an Asset Acquisition. The assets sold include inventory with a fair market value of $500, an adjusted FIFO basis of $300, and an adjusted LIFO basis of $200. ABC Corporation has adopted a plan of complete liquidation under Section 337. What gain (if any) must be reported by ABC Corporation?*

FIFO basis	$300
LIFO basis	200
Excess	$100

ABC Corporation will report $100 of ordinary income.

B.8　NET OPERATING LOSSES

A net operating loss occurs when a business has losses; that is, when its deductions exceed its revenue. Generally, a corporation that experiences a net operating loss may carryback such a loss to any of the three preceding taxable years to obtain a refund for taxes paid. If the company does not have sufficient taxable income in prior years to absorb the net operating loss, the company may carryforward the loss for up to 15 years.

It is fairly obvious that even if a corporation does not currently have a viable business, it is potentially worth something to another corporation if that corporation could use its net operating losses. The IRS has always been aware of this loophole and has substantially closed off the opportunity for companies to traffic in loss companies. Net operating losses of the target company can only be utilized if one of the four No Change in Basis Acquisition Methods are utilized to effect the transaction. These four are (1) Stock Acquisition, (2) Type A Reorganization, (3) Type B Reorganization, and (4) Type C Reorganization. Generally, in a Stock Acquisition the carryover of any net operating loss is governed by the following rule. If the acquiring company (technically the top 10 shareholders) (*a*) acquires 50 percent or more of the stock of the target either through a purchase from another unrelated party or through a decrease of the number of shares outstanding over a period dating back approximately two years, and (*b*) the company does not substantially carry on the same trade or business, then any net operating loss carryforward will not be allowed.[29] In any of the nontaxable reorganizations, a different set of rules apply. For these types of acquisitions, a limitation comes into play if the stockholders of the company with the net operating loss obtain less than 20 percent of the fair market value of the stock of the acquiring corporation outstanding after the transaction. If the stockholders receive anything less than the 20 percent, the net operating loss carryover is reduced by 5 percent for every percent under 20 percent that the stockholders receive.[30] Thus, if the stockholders receive only 10 percent of the stock of the acquiring company, the net operating loss carryover is cut in half.

B.9　MINIMUM TAX RULES AND THE CORPORATE TAX PREFERENCE CUTBACK

Individuals and corporations are subject to minimum tax rules in addition to their regular tax burden. These rules increase an individual's or corporation's total tax burden where the individual or corporation has availed itself of certain types of deductions which have been defined as tax preference items. Moreover, under present law corporations must reduce the benefit associated with certain deductions. These deductions are called corporate tax preference items, and the reduction of these deductions is called the corporate tax preference cutback. Due to the fact that some types of deductions are both corporate tax preference items and tax preference items for minimum tax purposes, special rules have been enacted to prevent a double impact of the two provisions.

B.901   Individual Alternative Minimum Tax

Individuals must pay a 20 percent tax on alternative minimum taxable income that exceeds an exemption amount to the extent that it exceeds their regular tax.

Alternative minimum taxable income is equal to adjusted gross income plus the sum of tax preference items less the sum of (*a*) the alternative tax net operating loss deduction, (*b*) the allowable alternative minimum tax itemized deductions, and (*c*) any accumulations distributed from a trust.

The exemption amount is (1) $20,000 for married taxpayers filing separately and trusts and estates, (2) $30,000 for single taxpayers, and (3) $40,000 for married taxpayers filing jointly and surviving spouses.

Tax preference items for individuals include (1) the excess of accelerated depreciation over straight-line depreciation on nonrecovery real property, (2) the excess of deductions for mining exploration and development costs over the amount that would have been deductible if such costs had been capitalized and amortized over 10 years, (3) the excess of deductions for research and experimental expenditures over the amount that would have been allowable if such expenditures had been capitalized and amortized over a 10-year period, (4) the excess of percentage depletion over the adjusted basis of the property at the end of the year, (5) the long-term capital gain deduction (excluding gain on the sale of a principal residence), (6) the excess of intangible drilling cost deductions over the deductions that would have been allowable had the costs been capitalized and amortized over the 10-year period beginning with the month in which production began, (7) the excess of the ACRS deduction for 15-year or 18-year real property over the straight-line deduction that would have been allowable, and (8) miscellaneous other preference items.

The regular tax is the income tax reduced by all credits except for the credit for withheld taxes, the earned income credit, and miscellaneous other credits.

B.902   Corporate Minimum Tax

Corporations (other than an S corporation) must pay a 15 percent tax on its tax preferences that exceed $10,000 to the extent that such tax exceeds its regular income tax liability.

Tax preference items for corporations include (1) the excess of accelerated depreciation over straight-line depreciation on nonrecovery property, (2) the excess of deductions for mining exploration and development costs over the amount that would have been deductible if such costs had been capitalized and amortized over 10 years, (3) the excess of deductions for research and experimental expenditures over the amount that would have been allowable if such expenditures had been capitalized and amortized over a 10-year period, (4) the excess of percentage depletion over the adjusted basis of the property at the end of the year, (5) 18/46 of a corporation's net capital gain, (6) the amount by which excess intangible drilling costs exceed the taxpayer's net income from oil, gas, and geothermal properties, (7) the excess of the ACRS deduction for 15-year or 18-year real property over the straight-line deduction that would have been allowable, and (8) miscellaneous other tax preference items.

A corporation's income tax liability for purposes of the minimum tax calculation includes its full income tax excluding the accumulated earnings tax, personal holding company tax, and miscellaneous other taxes less the sum of the following credits: the foreign tax credit, investment tax credit, targeted jobs tax credit, and miscellaneous other credits.

B.903   Corporate Tax Preference Cutback

Generally, corporations must reduce the benefit associated with certain deductions by 20 percent. These deductions are called corporate tax preference items, and the reduction of these deductions is called the corporate tax preference cutback. Corporate tax preference items include the following:

1. percentage depletion of iron ore and coal
2. rapid amortization of pollution control facilities
3. financial institutions bad debt reserves
4. gain on Section 1250 real property
5. financial institutions interest deductions on debt incurred to carry tax exempt bonds
6. deemed dividends from DISC's/FSC's
7. intangible drilling costs of integrated oil companies
8. mining exploration and development costs

B.10   ESTIMATED TAX PAYMENTS

Generally, a corporation must pay its estimated tax quarterly. The four payments are due on the 15th day of the 4th, 6th, 9th, and 12th months of the corporation's tax year. Given that most corporation's estimate of its tax liability changes during the year, corporations must recalculate their payments. The recalculation is made by subtracting the payments made to date, if any, from the estimated tax liability and dividing the resulting sum by the number of quarterly payments remaining to be made.

A corporation must pay a penalty tax if it underpays its estimated tax liability by more than 10 percent. The penalty tax is based on the prime rate and is adjusted semiannually. Certain exceptions exist to the penalty tax. No penalty tax will be imposed if payments made equal the smaller of (1) the tax for the preceeding year or (2) the tax calculated at current year's rates for the prior year's facts. These exceptions are not available for corporations with taxable income of at least $1 million in any one of the three preceeding years.

NOTES TO APPENDIX B

[1]IRC Section 11.

[2]See IRC Sections 1222 and 1223.

[3]IRC Section 1221.

[4]See IRC Sections 1245 (a)(1) and 1250 (a)(1).

[5]IRC Section 1202.

[6]IRC Section 1211.

[7]IRC Section 1201.

[8]IRC Section 1212 (b).

[9]IRC Sections 1211 (a) and 1212 (a).

[10]IRC Section 168.

[11]IRC Section 168 (c)(2).

[12]IRC Section 168 (b).

[13]IRC Section 168 (b)(3)(A).

[14]See Depreciation Guide for a general discussion of the Old Depreciation Systems.

[15]IRC Section 1245 (a)(5).

[16]IRC Section 46 (a)(2)(B).

[17]IRC Section 46 (a)(2)(E).

[18]IRC Section 44G (a)(2).

[19]IRC Section 48 (a)(1).

[20]IRC Section 48 (c)(2).

[21]IRC Section 48 (c)(7).

[22]IRC Section 48(c).

[23]IRC Section 38.

[24]IRC Section 46 (b).

[25]IRC Section 48 (q)(4).

[26]IRC Section 47 (a)(1).

[27]IRC Section 47 (a)(5).

[28]IRC Section 46 (a)(2)(c).

[29]IRC Section 382 (a).

[30]IRC Section 382 (b).

Appendix C

Accounting for an Acquisition

C.1 INTRODUCTION

As a general rule the author believes that the accounting treatment for an acquisition should not affect either the decision to acquire a target or the purchase price decision. Nevertheless, acquisition accounting is an important consideration in any transaction because the decision maker needs to understand the effect of the transaction on (1) the balance sheet of the acquiring company, (2) the acquiring company's earnings and earnings per share on a consolidated basis, and (3) the target's separate division or company results when they are actually reported. The second consideration is personally very key to the decision maker because the executive's future compensation is generally tied to the performance of the total company. The third consideration is important to the executive of the acquiring company who will be responsible for bringing in the results—assuming that the executive is presently employed by the acquiring company and involved somewhat in the negotiating process.

There are two accounting methods prescribed by the accounting profession for acquisitions: the **Pooling of Interests Method** and the **Purchase Method.**[1] The purpose of this chapter is to describe these mutually exclusive methods. It should be noted that the asset and liability values recorded for accounting purposes under either method typically differ from the values recorded for tax purposes (see paragraph C.202). Furthermore, the decision on which method to apply is made without regard for either the legal form of the transaction or the tax nature of the contemplated transaction.

Generally, most acquisitions in the 1980s are accounted for using the Purchase Method. Therefore, the primary focus of this chapter will be on this method. The Pooling of Interests Method is rarely used because of the stringent conditions associated with it.

C.2 PURCHASE METHOD OF ACCOUNTING

The Purchase Method of accounting is based on the theory that the accounting should follow the economic substance of the bargained transaction. Under the Purchase Method the assets and liabilities of the target company are recorded on the books of the acquiring company at their relative fair market values as of the acquisition date.

EXAMPLE CA   *ABC Corporation sells all of its assets and liabilities to XYZ Corporation in an Asset Acquisition for $1,700. What values would XYZ Corporation record for accounting purposes?*

	Asset and Liability Values Appearing on ABC's Books	Assumed Fair Market Values	Values Recorded on XYZ's Books
Accounts receivable	$100	$ 100	$ 100
Inventories	300	900	900
Property, plant, and equipment	700	1,100	1,100
Accounts payable and accrued expenses	(400)	(400)	(400)
	$700	$1,700	$1,700

In circumstances where the purchase price exceeds the net fair market value of the assets purchased and liabilities assumed, goodwill is recorded for accounting purposes. This "goodwill" figure is generally defined as an expectancy of earnings in excess of a normal return on the assets employed in a business. The expectancy of excess returns can come from any number of factors including location, trade secrets, brand names, reputation, or management skill. Any goodwill recorded must be amortized over its useful life which cannot exceed 40 years. Generally straight-line amortization is used, although another method may be employed if it is more appropriate. See paragraph 3.203c for a discussion of goodwill as it relates to taxes.

EXAMPLE CB   *Same facts as Example CA except that XYZ Corporation pays $2,000.*

EXAMPLE CB	Asset and Liability Values Appearing on ABC's Books	Assumed Fair Market Values	Values Recorded on XYZ's Books
Accounts receivable	$100	$ 100	$ 100
Inventories	300	900	900
Property, plant, and equipment	700	1,100	1,100
Goodwill			300*
Accounts payable and accrued expenses	(400)	(400)	(400)
	$700	$1,700	$2,000

*Purchase price less net fair market values of assets purchased and liabilities assumed ($2,000 − $1,700 = $300).

In cases where there is a bargain purchase (the purchase price is less than the net fair market value of the assets purchased and liabilities assumed), the values assigned to noncurrent assets (excluding long-term investments) are reduced by the difference between the purchase price and the net fair market value of the assets purchased and liabilities assumed.

EXAMPLE CC   *Same facts as Example CA except that XYZ Corporation pays $1,500.*

	Asset and Liability Values Appearing on ABC's Books	Assumed Fair Market Values	Values Recorded on XYZ's Books
Accounts receivable	$100	$ 100	$ 100
Inventories	300	900	900
Property, plant, and equipment	700	1,100	900*
Accounts payable and accrued expenses	(400)	(400)	(400)
	$700	$1,700	$1,500

*Fair market value of property, plant, and equipment less the difference between the net fair market value of the assets purchased and liabilities assumed and the purchase price ($1,100 − ($1,700 − $1,500) = $900).

In special situations where the noncurrent assets have been reduced to zero value and a bargain purchase still remains, then a deferred credit for the excess of the value of identifiable assets over the cost of the target company should be recorded. This deferred credit is sometimes referred to as "negative goodwill." This deferred credit appears on the balance sheet between long-term debt and stockholder's equity and is amortized into income.

EXAMPLE CD   *Same facts as Example CA except that XYZ Corporation pays* $500.

	Asset and Liability Values Appearing on ABC's Books	Assumed Fair Market Values	Values Recorded on XYZ's Books
Accounts receivable	$100	$ 100	$100
Inventories	300	900	900
Property, plant, and equipment	700	1,100	0*
Accounts payable and accrued expenses	(400)	(400)	(400)
Negative goodwill			(100)†
	$700	$1,700	$500

*Bargain purchase exists in amount greater than $1,100 so property, plant, and equipment reduced to $0.

†Bargain purchase remaining after reducing property, plant, and equipment to $0.

In the four preceding examples we have made two important assumptions: (1) that the cost of the acquisition and (2) the fair market values of all assets and liabilities were known. The first assumption is valid if the acquiring company paid cash. But what if other consideration is used to effect the transaction? How is the cost of the acquisition determined in that situation for accounting purposes? The basic rule in such cases is that cost is determined either by the fair value of the consideration given or by the fair value of the property acquired, whichever is more clearly evident. The problem of allocating the purchase price is the subject of the following paragraph.

C.201   Allocation of the Purchase Price

The problem of allocating the purchase price can be viewed as involving two questions: (1) How do we determine the fair value of specific assets and liabilities? (2) Having determined the assets and liabilities fair value, how do we allocate the purchase price among the acquired assets and liabilities?

C.201a   *Valuing Specific Assets and Liabilities*

In valuing specific assets and liabilities, the following techniques are applied:

Cash—valued dollar for dollar.

Marketable Securities—valued at current net realizable values.

Receivables—valued by discounting at appropriate current interest rates the amounts to be received less any necessary bad debt or collection costs.

Inventories—Finished goods and work in process inventories are valued at estimated selling prices less the sum of (*a*) costs to complete, (*b*) costs of disposal, and (*c*) a reasonable profit allowance for the completing and selling effort. Raw materials inventories are valued at current replacement cost.

Plant and Equipment—For that portion of plant and equipment to be used by the acquiring company, a value should be recorded equal to the current replacement costs for similar capacity unless the expected use by the acquirer indicates a lower value. In most instances this will mean that an appraised value will be used. Current replacement cost may be determined from a used asset market or from the new asset market less an estimated amount for depreciation. Plant and equipment that is to be sold should be valued at current net realizable value.

Intangible Assets—which can be identified should be valued at their appraised values.

Other Assets—including land, natural resources, and nonmarketable securities should be valued at appraised values.

Goodwill—is valued as indicated in paragraph C.2.

Liabilities—All liabilities (except deferred taxes) are to be valued by discounting at appropriate current interest rates the amounts to be paid.

C.201b General Allocation Rules

The general rules to follow in allocating the purchase price among the assets acquired and liabilities assumed are:

1. Assign value to all tangible and identifiable intangible assets based on their fair market values.
2. Assign value to liabilities assumed based on the present value of those liabilities.
3. If necessary, assign a value to goodwill equal to the difference between the purchase price and the net fair market value of the assets acquired and liabilities assumed.
4. If necessary, reduce the values assigned to noncurrent assets by a proportionate share of the difference between the purchase price and the net fair market value of the assets purchased and liabilities assumed. In unusual circumstances where the noncurrent assets have been reduced to zero value and a bargain purchase still remains, then record a deferred credit on the balance sheet.
5. If necessary, adjust the value assigned to assets to reflect the fact that certain assets will produce greater or lesser cash flows to the company because their tax basis differs from the assets fair mar-

ket value. In circumstances where an asset will produce different cash flows over a number of years, these cash flows should
be discounted at a reasonable rate.

6. Recompute the items described in (3) and (4) above.

In allocating the purchase price, Rule 5 above indicates that the effect of taxes should be considered. What does this mean? Basically
whenever the tax basis of an asset differs from the asset's fair market
value, the acquiring company will adjust the asset's fair market value
for the present value of the tax benefit or detriment associated with the
difference. See paragraph 3.203 for a discussion of how tax basis is determined in a New Cost Basis Acquisition Method. However, it must be
noted that a large number of acquisitions are recorded without adjust-
ing for the effect of taxes.

EXAMPLE CE   *ABC Corporation sells all of its assets to XYZ Corporation in
an Asset Acquisition. The assets sold include property, plant, and equipment
with a fair market value of $170 and a tax basis to the acquiring company of
$224. What should the book value of the property, plant and equipment be as-
suming a 50 percent tax rate?*

	Assumed Fair Market Value	*Tax Basis*	*Difference*
Property, plant, and equipment	$170	$224	$54

Calculation of Present Value of Tax Benefit

Year	*5-Year ACRS Depreciation Percentages*	*Difference*	*Depreciation Deductions*	*Taxes at 50 Percent*	*10 Percent Discount Factor*	*PV of Taxes*
1	.15	$54	$ 8.10	$4.05	.9091	$ 3.68
2	.22	54	11.88	5.94	.8264	4.91
3	.21	54	11.34	5.67	.7513	4.26
4	.21	54	11.34	5.67	.6830	3.87
5	.21	54	11.34	5.67	.6209	3.52
			$54.00			$20.24

Present value of tax benefit, say $20

Calculation of Book Value of Property, Plant, and Equipment

Fair market value	$170
Plus: Present value of tax benefit from excess of tax basis over fair market value	20
Book value	$190

*Based on the calculations above, XYZ Corporation will record property,
plant, and equipment on its accounting books at $190.*

EXAMPLE CF *Same as Example CE except that we analyze inventories that had a fair market value of $280 and a tax basis of $369.*

	Fair Market Value	Tax Basis	Difference
Inventories	$280	$369	$89

Here the book value will equal $324 (($280 ÷ (89 × 50% tax rate)) because presumably the inventory will be sold within one year.

The examples above dealt with a situation where the tax basis of assets did not significantly differ from their fair market values. In acquisitions where a No Change in Basis Acquisition Method is employed, one could expect to see significant adjustments for tax effects (see paragraph 3.3 for a discussion of these methods).

C.202   Differences between Book and Tax Allocations

Paragraph 3.203 outlines the valuation techniques used for tax purposes in allocating the purchase price in an Asset Acquisition and a 338 Transaction. These techniques differ from those described above for allocating value to assets for accounting reasons using the Purchase Method of accounting. An obvious result is that the allocations of the purchase price for book and tax typically do not agree.

EXAMPLE CG *ABC Corporation sells all of its assets to XYZ in an Asset Acquisition for $1,000. ABC's assets and their respective fair market values are listed below. What are their new tax basis and book values in the hands of XYZ? The tax basis of the assets in the hands of XYZ is $1,000. Since the purchase price exceeds the fair market value of ABC's assets a second tier, allocation must be performed. These calculations appear below. (Note that this example also appeared in paragraph 3.203.)*

Calculation of Tax Basis of Assets

Asset	(A) Fair Market Value	(B) Second Tier Allocation Calculation		(C) Allocation	(A) and (C) Tax Basis
Cash	$ 30				$ 30
Receivables	140*				140
Inventories	280	($280/$630) × ($1,000 − $800)	= $89		369
Property, plant, and equipment	170	($170/$630) × ($1,000 − $800)	= 54		224
Goodwill	180†	($180/$630) × ($1,000 − $800)	= 57		237
	$800				$1,000

*Equals gross value.

†The fair market value of goodwill is estimated for tax purposes, but for accounting purposes goodwill is calculated as described in paragraph C.2.

The fair market value of the tangible assets purchased is $620. We will assume that there are no identifiable intangible assets. If we also assume for the moment that the acquiring company has elected not to adjust asset values for any tax effects associated with different tax basis for the assets (see paragraph C.201b), XYZ Corporation will record the following values on its books:

Calculation of Book Values

Asset	Fair Market Value	Book Value
Cash	$ 30	$ 30
Receivables	140	140
Inventories	280	280
Property, plant, and equipment	170	170
Total	$ 620	
Purchase price	$1,000	
Less total above	620	
Goodwill	$ 380	380
		$1,000

These book values are compared to the tax basis of the assets below.

Comparison of Book Values and Tax Basis

	Book Value	Tax Basis	Difference
Cash	$ 30	$ 30	
Receivables	140	140	
Inventories	280	369	$(89)
Property, plant, and equipment	170	224	(54)
Goodwill	380	237	143
Total	$1,000	$1,000	$ 0

If however the acquiring company elects to adjust asset values for the tax effects associated with the difference in the tax basis of the assets, XYZ will record different values for book purposes. These calculations appear below. Note that for book purposes, goodwill amounts to $316—the difference between the purchase price and the net fair market value of the assets acquired adjusted for tax effects.

Calculation of Book Values

Asset	Fair Market Value	Adjustments for Tax Effects	Book Value
Cash	$ 30		$ 30
Receivables	140		140
Inventories	280	$44*	324
Property, plant, and equipment	170	20*	190
Total	$ 620	$64	$ 684

Calculation of Book Values (*concluded*)

Asset	Fair Market Value	Adjustments for Tax Effects	Book Value
Purchase price	$1,000		$1,000
Less total above	620		684
Goodwill	$ 380		$ 316

*See paragraph C.201b for calculation.

Comparison of Book Values and Tax Basis

	Book Value	Tax Basis	Difference
Cash	$ 30	$ 30	
Receivables	140	140	
Inventories	324	369	$(45)
Property, plant, and equipment	190	224	(34)
Goodwill	316	237	79
Total	$1,000	$1,000	$ 0

EXAMPLE CH   *Same as Example CG except the purchase price is $500. The tax basis of the assets in the hands of XYZ is $500. Since the purchase price is less than the fair market value of ABC's assets, a second tier allocation must be performed. The calculations are as follows:*

Calculation of Tax Basis of Assets

Asset	(A) Fair Market Value	(B) Second Tier Allocation Calculation	(C) Allocation	(A) and (C) Tax Basis
Cash	$ 30			$ 30
Receivables	140*			140
Inventories	280	($280/$630) × ($500 − $800)	= $(133)	147
Property, plant, and equipment	170	($170/$630) × ($500 − $800)	= (81)	89
Goodwill	180	($180/$630) × ($500 − $800)	= (86)	94
	$800			$500

*Equals gross value.

The fair market value of the tangible assets purchased is $620. We will assume that there are no identifiable intangible assets. If we also assume for the moment that the acquiring company has elected not to adjust asset values for any tax effects associated with different tax basis for the assets (see paragraph C.201b), XYZ Corporation will record the following values on its books:

Calculation of Book Values

Asset	Fair Market Value	Adjustment for Negative Goodwill	Book Value
Cash	$ 30		$ 30
Receivables	140		140
Inventories	280		280
Property, plant, and equipment	170	$(120)	50
Total	$ 620		

Purchase price	500	
Less total above	620	
Negative goodwill	$(120)	$500

These book values are compared to the tax basis of the assets below.

Comparison of Book Values and Tax Basis

	Book Value	Tax Basis	Difference
Cash	$ 30	$ 30	
Receivables	140	140	
Inventories	280	147	$133
Property, plant, and equipment	50	89	(39)
Goodwill	0	94	(94)
Total	$500	$500	$ 0

If, however, the acquiring company elects to adjust asset values for the tax effects associated with the difference in the tax basis of the assets, XYZ will record different values for book purposes. These calculations appear below. Note that for book purposes, negative goodwill amounts to $24—after adjusting for tax effects. Thus, property, plant, and equipment is reduced by that amount in determining book values.

Calculation of Book Values

Asset	Fair Market Value	Adjustment for Tax Effects	Sub-total	Adjustment for Negative Goodwill	Book Value
Cash	$ 30		$ 30		$ 30
Receivables	140		140		140
Inventories	280	$(66)*	214		214
Property, plant, and equipment	170	(30)†	140	$(24)	116
Total	$620	$ 64	$524		$500

*(Fair market value − Tax basis) × Tax rate. ($280 − $147) × 50% = $66.

†Assuming all property is five-year ACRS property, the proper adjustment is $30 calculated below.

Year	ACRS Percent	Difference	Depreciation Deductions	Taxes at 50 Percent	10 Percent Discount Factor	PV of Taxes
1	0.15	$81*	$12.15	$6.08	0.9091	$ 5.53
2	0.22	81	17.82	8.92	0.8264	7.33
3	0.21	81	17.01	8.50	0.7513	6.39
4	0.21	81	17.01	8.50	0.6830	5.81
5	0.21	81	17.01	8.50	0.6209	5.28
			$81.00			$30.38
			Present value of tax benefit, say,			$30.00

*Fair market value of plant, property, and equipment less tax basis ($170 − $89 = $81).

The resulting book values and tax basis of the assets are compared below.

Comparison of Book Values and Tax Basis

	Book Value	Tax Basis	Difference
Cash	$ 30	$ 30	
Receivables	140	140	
Inventories	214	147	$ 67
Property, plant, and equipment	116	89	27
Goodwill	0	94	(94)
Total	$500	$500	$ 0

Although the book and tax differences are substantial in the examples, they pale by comparison to the differences between book and tax values that result when one uses the Purchase Method of accounting in an acquisition where the transaction is effected using a No Change in Basis Acquisition Method (see paragraph 3.3 for listing of four types of No Change in Basis Acquisition Methods). In acquisitions effected under those methods, the tax basis of the assets of the target do not change, yet the fair market values of the assets of the target are recorded on the books of the acquiring company; sometimes net of the tax benefits that are lost as a result of not being able to step up the tax basis of the assets of the target to their fair market values.

C.203   Financial Statement Disclosure

If the Purchase Method of accounting is used to record an acquisition, the notes to the financial statements of the acquiring company must describe the target, the date it was acquired, the cost of the acquisition including the types of consideration exchanged, the amount of any goodwill resulting from the transaction, and any contingent payments, options, or commitments associated with the acquisition. Furthermore, the acquiring company must disclose the following results of operation on a pro forma basis: (1) operating results for the current period assuming the acquisition took place at the beginning of the period: and (2) if comparative financial statements are presented, operating results for the immediately preceding period assuming the transaction had been effected at the beginning of that period. Pro forma presentation of the results of operations of any other prior periods is not permitted. The pro forma information disclosed must include revenue, income before extraordinary items, net income, and earnings per share.

C.3   POOLING OF INTERESTS METHOD

The Pooling of Interests Method of accounting is based on the assumption that certain transactions are merely arrangements between stockholder groups to exchange equity securities. Therefore, the only accounting adjustment to record in these situations is a change in the ownership interests of the stockholders. This is effected by eliminating the capital stock of the target company and recording the new stock issued by the acquiring company to the target company's shareholders. Otherwise, the acquiring company and the target company merely combine assets and liabilities at their historical book values on the acquisition date.

EXAMPLE CI   *XYZ Corporation agrees to purchase ABC Corporation in a Type B Reorganization. XYZ will exchange one share of its common stock for every share of ABC Corporation outstanding. We will assume that the transaction meets all the requirements for Pooling of Interests treatment specified in paragraph C.301 and that the company's balance sheets before the transaction are as follows:*

	Book Values	
	XYZ	ABC
Cash and accounts receivable	$ 500	$ 100
Inventories	700	300
Property, plant, and equipment	2,000	700
Total assets	$3,200	$1,100
Accounts payable and accrued expenses	$ 700	$ 400
Common stock (par $1)	250	70
Contributed capital in excess of par value	1,250	530
Retained earnings	1,000	100
Stockholders equity	2,500	700
Total liabilities and stockholders equity	$3,200	$1,100

The acquiring company would record the investment in ABC Corporation on its books on the date of the transaction in the amount of $700. The journal entry that XYZ would record is:

	Debit	Credit
Investment in ABC Corporation	70	
Common Stock (par $1)		70

However the consolidated balance sheet of the entities would eliminate this investment against ABC's stockholders' equity accounts.

Consolidation Worksheet

	Book Values		Eliminations		XYZ and ABC
	XYZ	ABC	Debit	Credit	Consolidated
Cash and Accounts receivable	$ 500	$ 100			$ 600
Inventories	700	300			1,000
Investment in ABC Corporation	70			$70	
Property, plant, and equipment	2,000	700			2,700
Total assets	$3,270	$1,100			$4,300
Accounts payable and accrued expenses	$ 700	$ 400			$1,100
Common stock (par $1)	320	70	$ 70		320
Contributed capital in excess of par value	1,250	530			1,780
Retained earnings	1,000	100	100		1,000
Stockholders equity	2,570	700			3,200
Total liabilities and stockholders equity	$3,270	$1,100			$4,300

C.301 Criteria for Pooling

Accounting Principles Board Opinion No. 16, "Business Combinations," prescribes 12 specific criteria for a pooling. If any of the criteria are not met, the transaction must be accounted for using the Purchase Method. The criteria are classified into three categories: (*a*) attributes of the combining companies. (*b*) manner of combining the interests, and (*c*) absence of planned transactions.

Attributes of the Combining Companies

1. Each of the combining companies must be autonomous and must not have been a division or subsidiary of another corporation for two years prior to the initiation of the plan of combination. A new enterprise generally meets this requirement unless it is a successor to part or all of an entity that does not meet the requirement.

2. The combining entities must be independent of the other combining entities. This means that a combining entity can hold no more than a 10 percent interest in the outstanding voting common stock of another combining entity.

Manner of Combining the Interests

3. The combination must be accomplished within one year according to a specific plan or by a single transaction.

4. The surviving corporation must issue only common stock with rights identical to those of the majority of its outstanding voting common stock in exchange for substantially all of the voting common stock of the other combining entities at the date the plan of combination is consummated. For purposes of this requirement, a class of stock that has voting control is the majority class. Furthermore, substantially all of the voting common stock means 90 percent or more.

5. None of the combining entities may change the equity interest of the voting common stock through exchanges, retirements, issuances, or distributions in contemplation of effecting the combination.

6. Any of the combining entities may reacquire shares of voting common stock, but only if the purpose is unrelated to the business combination. Furthermore, after the plan of combination is initiated, only a normal number of shares may be so acquired.

7. Each individual common shareholder who exchanges stock must receive a voting common stock interest exactly in proportion to its relative voting common stock interest before the transaction.

8. The voting rights of the stockholders of any of the combined entities cannot be deprived or restricted as part of the plan of combination.

9. The combination must be resolved at the date the plan of combination is consummated. No provision is allowed for the issuance of securities or other consideration.

Absence of Planned Transactions

10. The combined entity cannot agree directly or indirectly to retire or reacquire any or part of the common stock issued to effect the combination.

11. The combined enterprise cannot enter into other financial arrangements for the benefit of the former stockholders of a combining enterprise, such as a guaranty of loans secured by stock issued in the combination, that in effect negates the exchange of equity securities.

12. The combined enterprise cannot intend or plan to dispose of a significant part of the assets of the combining enterprises within two years after the combination, other than disposals in the ordinary course of business of the formerly separate enterprises and to eliminate duplicate facilities or excess capacity.

C.302 Financial Statement Disclosure

Any company that applies the Pooling of Interests Method of accounting to a combination must report results of operations for the period in which the combination occurs as though the enterprises had been combined as of the beginning of the period. Furthermore, balance sheets and other financial information of the separate enterprises as of the beginning of the period must be presented as though the companies had been combined at that date. Any financial statements and financial information of the separate enterprises presented for prior years must also be restated on a combined basis to furnish comparative information. All restated financial statements and financial summaries must indicate clearly that financial data is on a combined basis.

The notes to the financial statements of a combined enterprise must disclose a description of the combined entities, detailed information (including for example, revenue, extraordinary items and net income) on the results of operations of the previously separate companies for the period before the combination that are included in current combined net income and miscellaneous other information.

NOTES TO APPENDIX C

[1]See *Accounting Principles Board Opinion No. 16,* "Accounting for Business Combinations" (New York: American Institute of Certified Public Accountants, 1970).

REFERENCES FOR APPENDIX C

Accounting Principles Board Opinion No. 16, "Accounting for Business Combinations." New York: American Institute of Certified Public Accountants, 1970.

Accounting Principles Board Opinion No. 17, "Accounting for Intangibles." New York: American Institute of Certified Public Accountants, 1970.

Defliese, Philip L., Kenneth P. Johnson, and Roderick K. MacLeod. *Montgomery's Auditing,* 9th ed. 669–703. New York: John Wiley & Sons, 1975.

Interpretations of APB Opinion Nos. 16 and 17, 5th ed. Arthur Anderson & Co., 1981.

Pahler, Arnold J., and Joseph E. Mori. *Advanced Accounting: Concepts and Practice,* 37–234, New York: Harcourt Brace Jovanovich, Inc., 1981.

Wendell, Paul J. *Corporate Controller's Manual,* chaps. 30–33. Boston, Mass.: Warren, Gorham & Lamont, Inc., 1981.

Index